WHY BEYOND HY.

Only 20 minutes per day for 30 days can turn you into a skilled, practicing psychic. This book takes you beyond hypnosis to show you how to create your own reality, how you can reshape your own life and the lives of others, and ultimately the world, and beyond what we call this world.

Beyond Hypnosis will open you to powers such as *telepathic communication, astral travel, communication with non-physical sources,* and other psychic phenomena. Some are extremely practical—such as the right choice of action in daily affairs, improving your life in measurable ways.

You are responsible for making both personal and collective choices every day. You can learn to make your choices become reality. You alone can change any aspect of your life.

The four elements necessary for achievement are:
1) **Have a wish, i.e. desire.**
2) **Create the dream, i.e. visualize.**
3) **Release the dream to Higher Consciousness while still retaining the visualization.**
4) **Take constructive action, i.e. take control and direct your dream.**

You will learn many specific abilities, develop several very real sources of knowledge, and learn to apply your knowledge and skill for self-betterment and even world betterment.

YES, YOU CAN CHANGE ANY ASPECT OF YOUR LIFE THAT YOU REALLY WANT TO, AND THIS BOOK SHOWS YOU HOW TO DISCOVER YOUR *TRUE WILL* AND MAKE IT HAPPEN!

About the Author

WILLIAM W. HEWITT has practiced clinical hypnosis professionally since 1972. He has his own practice in Colorado. He is a Professional Member of the American Association of Professional Hypnotherapists. He is actively involved in lecturing in the areas of hypnosis, psychic phenomena, mind control, and other subjects. He has also been a technical writer for the past 23 years in the areas of data processing, computers, mining, management procedures, medical equipment, and other fields of interest. Mr. Hewitt is a professional astrologer and a member of the American Federation of Astrologers. He is also a graduate of the Silva Mind Control basic and graduate courses. He uses self-hypnosis daily to enable him to quickly learn the technicalities and details needed for his technical writing assignments.

To Write to the Author

We cannot guarantee that every letter written to the author can be answered, but all will be forwarded to them. Both the author and the publisher appreciate hearing from readers, learning of your enjoyment and benefit from this book. Llewellyn also publishes a bi-monthly news magazine with news and reviews of practical esoteric studies and articles helpful to the student, and some readers' questions and comments to the author may be answered through this magazine's columns if permission to do so is included in the original letter. The author sometimes participates in seminars and workshops, and dates and places are announced in *The Llewellyn New Times*. To write to the author, or to ask a question, write to:

William W. Hewitt
c/o THE LLEWELLYN NEW TIMES
P.O. Box 64383-305, St. Paul, MN 55164-0383, U.S.A.
Please enclose a self-addressed, stamped envelope for reply, or $1.00 to cover costs.

ABOUT LLEWELLYN'S SELF-IMPROVEMENT SERIES

Today, everything is moving fast. Cars and jets move faster. Computers work at ever-increasing speeds. It seems hard to keep up with the changes in the world around us. In fact, the world is moving so fast around us that if you stay where you are, you are actually falling behind.

Unfortunately, we do not have the luxury of time afforded to people a mere fifty years ago. We need to progress rapidly without wasted time or effort. This is where **Llewellyn's Self-Improvement** series comes in.

This series gives you a direct opportunity for personal growth and development—at your own speed, on your own time.

*This series helps you to achieve self-growth through practical, step-by-step guidance from people who have **mastered** the techniques they are sharing.*

This series will allow you to improve your innate abilities, always showing how they can be used in a practical, down-to-earth context.

The results can be phenomenal! Not only will you be able to "keep up with the pack," but you will be able to far outdistance those who are merely trying to keep up. **Llewellyn's Self-Improvement Series** will help you develop a new, more positive, more successful, style of living!

Congratulations on choosing this book! You are now starting on the road to a better, happier, more productive life.

Other Books by William Hewitt

Hypnosis: A Power Program for Self-Improvement,
   Changing Your Life and Helping Others
Tea Leaf Reading
Astrology forBeginners

Tapes by William Hewitt

Llewellyn offers a series of audio tapes to help you with a
variety of problems, like relaxation, weight control, success and other topics. Please write for our catalog or see
the ad pages in the back of this book for a complete list.

Forthcoming

The Art of Self-Talk
Build a Bridge to Tomorrow

Llewellyn's Self-Improvement Series

BEYOND HYPNOSIS

William W. Hewitt

1992
Llewellyn Publications
St. Paul, Minnesota 55164-0383, U.S.A.

FIRST EDITION
Fifth Printing, 1992

Cover Photo © ORION/FPG International

Library of Congress Cataloging-in-Publication Data
  Hewitt, William W., 1929–
    Beyond hypnosis
        p.   cm. — (Llewellyn's self-improvement series)
      ISBN 0–87542–305–1
    1. Psychical research. 2. Occult sciences. I Title. II. Series
  BF1031.H357 1957   87–45733
  133.8   CIP

Llewellyn Publications
A Division of Llewellyn Worldwide, Ltd.
P.O. Box 64383, St. Paul, MN 55164-0383

Choices, once executed, cannot be erased.
This book is dedicated to all people who
execute choices that make the world a
better place for their having been here.

CHOICES

There is only one,
Be it a moment
Or an eternity.
And when all is done,
One cannot lament
What's there for all to see.

Our battle goes on,
And choices are drawn
To direct our attack.
And when all is done,
On that final dawn
Nothing can we take back.

CONTENTS

INTRODUCTION

This book will take you into the dimension of psychic awareness and tell you how to use this dimension in constructive ways for the benefit of yourself, others, and ultimately the entire society.

The psychic dimension is extremely powerful and useful. It is obtainable by everyone who is willing to exercise the self-discipline and spend a small amount of time each day to learn and practice their innate psychic ability. Everyone has psychic ability; it is part of one's birthright. Most people either ignore this marvelous gift or are unaware of its presence and how to use it.

Chapter 5 is the heart of this book. This chapter delineates in detail a 30-session self-help how-to program for removing the veil that now curtains your psychic awareness from your conscious awareness. Your psychic awareness is then honed to a fine skill through a series of mental exercises. For the most part only about 20 minutes per session are required. At the end of your 30 sessions of self-training, you will be a skilled, practicing psychic.

This program is designed so that you can use it all by yourself; all you need is a cassette tape recorder and a few inexpensive blank tapes. Of course, if you want to pursue

1

this training with someone else, so much the better. It is especially good for husband and wife, close friends, or even small close-knit groups. The reinforcement that partners bring to each other is invaluable.

Psychic power is so effective that it would be irresponsible to just launch into developing the power without first having a good understanding of yourself, life, interaction with others, responsibility, choices, rights, and much more. Therefore, the chapters preceding Chapter 5 contain the preparatory knowledge you need to ensure your success in a responsible way as a citizen of the universe.

Chapter 6 is a special chapter for graduates . . . a graduate being a person who completes the 30-session program exactly as it is described in Chapter 5. In the 'graduate' chapter I show you many ways you can begin to immediately start using your new-found psychic powers every day so you can make psychic practice an automatic method of bringing enjoyment, achievement, and benefit into your life and the lives of other.

The last chapter, *The Ultimate*, brings into focus why your psychic development is so very important *now*.

Throughout the book I include actual experiences I have had to show some of the infinite aspects of psychic experience and use of psychic ability. The purpose is to help you recognize your own psychic experiences when they occur.

Many people know all the 'buzz words' associated with psychic phenomena such as: clairvoyance; clairaudience; astral travel; altered states; telepathy; psychokinesis, etc. But few really understand what it is all about. That is like knowing the price of everything, but the value of nothing. This book brings you the value, not a vocabulary of buzz words.

William Hewitt

CHAPTER 1

YOU

This book is about *you*. You personally. How you interact with others and your environment. How you determine your own destiny, your own success or failure. How you can deliberately choose to alter your life for the better, and then make it happen.

This book is about *you*. You collectively as a family unit. How your members can act in harmony or disharmony. How you can be mutually constructive or destructive. How all of you can deliberately choose the direction of your family and make it happen.

This book is about *you*. You collectively as a corporation or business. How you collectively determine whether you become a good, constructive corporate citizen that strengthens the nation or a corporate leech on society.

This book is about *you*. You collectively as a nation. How you affect your fellow citizens and the other nations of the world. How you can choose to make a constructive difference, and then make it happen.

In all of these discussions about *YOU*, only one you is really being discussed . . . you personally . . . you the individual. It is about your choices and your actions. It is about your responsibilities and your innate power to execute those responsibilities.

This is a how-to book. How to enrich your life and the entire world. All in one fell swoop? Yes, all in one fell swoop!

You do make a difference. For better or worse, you do make an important, real, measurable difference.

What? You say you have heard this all before? Perhaps so. Perhaps you heard without understanding, or at least without full understanding. Perhaps you heard, but it wasn't really clear. Perhaps you could benefit by hearing it again in different words from a different perspective, and at a different point in your life.

There probably won't be anything startlingly new in this book. And yet, the ideas presented and thoughts expressed may well be a refreshingly new approach that will jingle something deep inside you and get you off dead center. In other words, they'll give you a mental kick in the rear to propel you into action to enrich your life—to go from the most simple, mundane events to awesome, earth-shaking events.

Take a chance. Read on. It will only take a couple hours of your time, and it may very well be the most beneficial time you have spent up to this point in your life. This book very simply shows you what needs to be done, and shows you how to do it. The actual "doing it," of course, is entirely up to you. That is your choice.

If you want a better life for yourself, your children, your friends, for everyone, this book is for you. If you really don't give a hoot one way or the other, this book is for you, too, because you just might develop a new perspective that will open up new, exciting vistas beyond your current imagination.

Imagine with me for a moment. Imagine that each element of our Earth and its inhabitants is represented by one tiny, beautifully colored brick. Each of these billions of tiny bricks is carefully cemented into place to form the Earth. Each brick supports other bricks, and each brick is in turn supported by other bricks.

Now imagine you are standing in space observing this creation of bricks. What do you see? You see a perfect globe of masonry work. The billions of colored bricks are blended in perfect mutual support to form a globe that is exquisitely beautiful, structurally sound, and incredibly strong. It is as perfect as anything you have ever seen.

Imagine now that someone with a hammer and chisel has destroyed one of those tiny bricks, leaving a small hole in the globe. Is not the structure less sound now? By only a tiny degree to be sure, but nonetheless weakened. This tiny scar also has diminished the beauty of the globe by some small degree.

Now someone with a jackhammer goes to work on this magnificent structure and destroys millions of bricks here and there all over the globe, leaving it horribly pockmarked with holes. The beauty has been horribly damaged. In some places, the structure is downright ugly. The strength has been sapped. Millions of bricks are no longer adequately supported so that any additional stress could cause them to crumble. Sufficient stress with sufficient additional crumbling could cause the entire globe to collapse and cease to exist.

Could the destruction of this beautiful brick globe have been prevented? Of course! How? Simply by not weakening or destroying the individual bricks. Or at least by not weakening such massive numbers of bricks as to significantly threaten the stability of the entire structure.

"Simpleton!" you shout. "That is obvious! What does that have to do with me? You said this book was about me and how I can enrich my life, yet you talk about bricks. What is the point?"

The point is that *you are one of those tiny bricks.* Every human being on the face of this Earth is one of those tiny bricks.

Our world is not a society of bricks and cement as used in my metaphor. It is a society of individual people. We are the bricks of our world, and the strength and beauty of that world depends very directly on each of us. You personally influence the soundness of our world in some way.

"You've got to be kidding. I'm just a little old lady on social security. My influence is zip!"

"Get off it, Mac! I drive a taxi in the Big Apple. My biggest influence is in deciding which route to take across Manhattan."

"I'm just a freshman in high school. I can't even get elected class president let alone anything really important."

No, I am not mistaken. I am talking about *you*, the little old lady, and *you*, the taxi driver, and *you* the student. Every YOU in the world—regardless of social position, intelligence level, economic level, race, religion, color, political bent, or nationality—is the subject I am addressing. YOU are all equally important; no one more so, nor less so, than the other. Each of you has power beyond your wildest imagination. And your use or misuse of that power determines whether you prevent the world from being pockmarked or whether you help in pockmarking the world.

"Wars pockmark the world," you say, "and I do not condone wars!"

True, war is one of a great many things that pockmark the world. But war is not the root cause.

Hunger and famine also are a pockmark, but they are not the root cause. True, hunger exists on a gigantic scale, but it doesn't have to.

Political injustice is a pockmark, but it is not the root cause.

I could go on to list hundreds of pockmarks that weaken our entire society, but I'll leave it to you to complete the list while you expand your awareness as we progress through this book together.

Several times I referred to a root cause. What is the root cause? Are you ready for this? *You* are the root cause.

"Hold on! You've gone too far now. I've never lifted a finger in anger against any man. Don't blame me for the world's troubles!"

First of all, I don't blame anyone. This book is about *what is* . . . it is about truth. In truth, there is no blame . . . there just *is*.

Secondly, you don't have to personally do something in order to be responsible for an undesirable result. If you do not do something that you could have, then you must bear responsibility for the result.

Remember this axiom: "All that it takes for evil to exist is for good people to do nothing."

Most of the people in the world are good, and all can potentially be good if they so choose. Yet the world is horribly pockmarked. Why?

Because those who can choose to correct or prevent the problems don't. In all fairness, they don't because of ignorance. They don't know they have a choice, and they don't know they have the power.

Here and now I tell you—you do have a choice, and you do have the power. This book will explore choices and show you how to develop and exercise your power.

Hitler brought massive destruction into the world because he was supported by millions of bricks (individuals) who didn't know they had a choice and didn't know how to exercise their innate power. Finally, masses of righteous men and women became so outraged that they fought back and created more destruction in order to stop Hitler. It had to be done. But the truly sad thing is that the situation need not have existed in the first place.

Remember, a brick must be supported by other bricks in order to create a structure. Good bricks make a good structure. Defective bricks make a defective structure. You are a brick. We all are bricks. However, there is a significant difference. A masonry brick has no choice about whether it will be defective or not; the skill of the brickmaker or external circumstances determine that. The masonry brick has no choice about what kind of structure it supports; it must support wherever it is put.

We are different. We human bricks always have a choice about the quality of our lives and about our role in the structure called society. The problems often occur because we don't realize that we indeed do have a choice and indeed do have the power to exercise our choices and determine our own destiny.

You are a brick. A brick with free will and power. This book will show you how to unleash your choices and power so you can build your life into the happy, successful, harmonious, beautiful structure you want. In turn, you will learn how to build family, corporate, national and international structures right from the comfort of your own home, so to speak. Am I kidding? No. This is real. This is truth. All you need to do is recognize the truth and use it . . . flow with it . . . harmonize with it . . . embrace it, and in so doing change the world for the better.

Are you completely happy? Probably not. The truth is you do not have to be unhappy.

Is there hatred in the world? Yes. The truth is there doesn't have to be.

There is nothing in the world that exists without us, either individually or collectively, having caused it. There is nothing in the world that cannot be corrected or changed if we, either individually or collectively, decide to do it.

How to do it is fairly simple, but it requires unwavering

individual commitment. This book can get you started, but the commitment is up to you.

About this point, you probably anticipate that I am about to unload some platitudes on you such as, "Write to your congressman about what you want" or "Exercise your right to vote." Those things are important, of course, but this book has nothing to do with those kinds of actions or solutions. This book is going to take you into a realm of power that is truly awesome. I am going to take you beyond hypnosis, and show you how you can create your own reality. How you can help reshape your life and the lives of others and ultimately the world, and beyond what we call the world.

For those readers who have read my previous book, *Hypnosis*, this book, *Beyond Hypnosis*, offers you ways to open doors to experiences you never thought really existed.

Some of the experiences available to you are quite esoteric, such as: telepathic communications; astral travel; direct communication with nonphysical intelligent sources; psychic phenomena; and all the others that fall under the general category of paranormal experience. A portion of this book deals with these uses of your mind.

Some of the experiences available to you are quite practical, such as: taking the most beneficial action in day-to-day affairs; making better choices in all avenues of your daily life; learning how to flow with energy in such a way as to actually cause improvement in your life in real, measurable ways. Much of this book is devoted to the practical uses of your mind because we are living this life right now, and this is most important to understand and deal with.

The esoteric and thè practical are not that far apart . . . they are quite compatible . . . and there is a chapter on blending these two into one extremely powerful creative force.

CHAPTER 2

CHOICES

You are really two people. One is the individual you, the one who makes hundreds of daily choices about the governing of your life. These choices run the gamut from which pair of shoes to wear, what to eat, whether or not to seek a new job, etc. These are those personal choices that directly, and often immediately, affect you. You are totally responsible for these choices, and you personally reap the results of your choices. If you make a poor choice, you reap an undesirable result. If you make a good choice, you reap a desirable result. It is your choice, and you are responsible.

Wouldn't it be nice if you made more good choices and fewer poor choices? Wouldn't it be nicer still if you made all good choices and no poor choices? Wouldn't it be nice if there were a way to stack the odds in your favor for making only good choices?

Good news! There is a way to stack the odds in your favor so you make better choices. In fact, you can go beyond this and actually make choices and then make them become reality. No longer do you have to hope things will turn out OK; you can now make them turn out OK. The bulk of this book is devoted to teaching you how to do just that.

The second you is a collective you. That is, you are

part of a group of other people who are jointly directing your mental energies and making choices for a common goal. This might be simply a family unit where you are jointly planning a vacation. Here you all know each other and have a very personal goal. The outcome of your choice will be immediately felt, and it will affect each of you directly and personally.

Another collective you might be part of a group that you don't even know. For example, you vote for candidate X in a national election. You have made a choice harmonious with the millions of others who also vote for candidate X. You don't even know the other people who made the same choice. And how this choice may or may not affect you becomes more complex than a personal choice such as whether or not to see a movie today. This subject will be explored in more detail later.

These "collective you" choices are every bit as important as your "individual you" choices. You are responsible for your collective choices and their results.

And the additional good news is that you can stack the odds in your favor in these "collective you" choices also. This book will get you started in understanding how.

If you are not pleased with who you are, where you are, what you are doing, or where you seem to be heading, don't think others are responsible. You alone are responsible. And you can change any aspect of your life that you really want to. The key is "really want to." Most people wish things were different, but that is as far as it goes. They do not really want to cause a change strongly enough. Mere wishing is not enough. As my late beloved father used to say, "Put your wishes in one hand and put garbage in the other. Watch and see which fills up first." So if you rely just on wishing, you are going to collect garbage in your life.

A wish, however, is a good beginning for improve-

ment as long as you are willing to advance b[...]
ing stage. Take your wish, turn it into a clearly d[...]
structive dream, release that dream to higher int[...]
for results, and then follow up with the best constru[...]
action you can to make the dream come true. And alway[...]
hold that dream strongly in your mind as you pursue your
actions to create your reality.

You say you have lost your left arm in an auto accident
and wish you had the arm back. How can you turn that wish
into reality? Well, literally you cannot grow another arm
because that is contrary to physical law. Starfish can grow
new arms to replace lost ones, but human beings cannot.
That is universal law. This brings up a very important rule:
whatever you want to become reality in your life must be in
harmony with universal law. That *is* the law. That is truth.
That is just the way it is.

You might be able to get some sort of artificial arm
replacement. Or you might be able to hire someone to help
you so they, in effect, become another arm. But you cannot
physically grow another arm. For your wishes to progress
to reality they must follow universal law.

Let me cite an example of how wishes can become
reality.

Dolly Parton lived in abject poverty in the hills of Tennessee. Dolly had a wish. She wished she could be rich and
famous and do something good in the world.

Then Dolly created her clearly defined, constructive
dream from her wish. She analyzed what she had to offer.
She could sing, play the guitar, and compose lyrics. She had
a rich family heritage of love and of vivid experiences of
poverty. So she dreamed of becoming a singer and com-
poser of country music. She released this dream to her
higher intelligence, all the while keeping it foremost in her
vision. Then she went to Nashville and pounded on doors,
auditioned, made demo records, etc. In short, she did every-

nk of to make her dream

ecame rich and famous and
e world through her music,
dhood experiences. If she had
till be in the Tennessee moun-

are necessary for achievement:
sire).
m (visualize).
3. Rel..... ream to higher intelligence (faith
and commit.ment) while still retaining the visualization.
4. Take constructive action (take control and direct
your dream).

Or, you could write the formula like this:
Desire + dream + faith + commitment + action
= success

Up to this point, this book does not differ substantially
from many other so-called "success" books. We have established the premise that you can change virtually anything in your world that you wish to change, and have
stated some basic conditions for creating change. Now we
depart into a different dimension in order to implement the
changes we want.

The dimension we are going to enter is one called
altered states of consciousness into a realm I call *beyond
hypnosis.*

RESPONSIBILITY

We are all born involved
If we like it or not;
And choosing to ignore
Does not make us absolved
From sustaining the blot
Of not having done more.

All our lives interlace
in delicate balance;
And our charge in living
is to die in the grace
Of having helped enhance
Life by our own giving.

Responsibility
is ours by right of birth;
And choosing to do or not
When it comes to our duty
Determines our worth
in life's daily plot.

CHAPTER 3

THE ALTERED STATE

Hypnosis is the name for a procedure that enables you to alter your state of consciousness so you can achieve some desirable goal. Meditation is another name for a procedure that enables you to alter your state of consciousness to achieve some desirable goal. Prayer is another name. Going to level, another. And there are any number of other names. All work quite well if you understand what you are doing and practice faithfully.

In this book, I will dispense with all the "names" and just talk about altered states and how you can learn to achieve them. And most importantly, what purpose you can invoke in an altered state of mind.

At the onset, I want to establish a clear understanding of what altered states are all about. There are two types of altered states: a harmful one, and a beneficial one.

The harmful altered state is induced by alcohol or drugs. In this state, you are **not** in control even though you have the delusion that you are. You are in physical and mental danger. Your health is endangered. You can possibly become "possessed" by another intelligent energy much to your horror. Please do not experiment with this type of mind altering because you have everything to lose, and

17

absolutely nothing to gain. This book does not teach or advocate anything that is harmful.

The highly beneficial altered state is the one that this book is all about. We are designed by our Creator to have altered states of consciousness as part of our innate ability to use for our benefit. We experience these altered states every day of our lives quite spontaneously (more on this shortly). What we are going to discuss is how to achieve the altered state when we want to, and then use that opportunity to invoke some desired change in our life. This beneficial altered state is achieved without the use of any drugs, medicines, etc. It is achieved by using your own natural ability to control your own mind.

This book intends to enable you to become independent, rather than dependent, and to be completely in control of your own life at all times in concert with the choices you decide for yourself. No longer do you need to be subjected to the whims and desires of others. No longer do you need to give up part of your identity, your dreams, your goals, to satisfy what someone else wants of you.

Did you ever wonder why some marriages are a bed of disharmony, contention, unhappiness, and lack of fulfillment? Yet other marriages are harmonious, happy, and fulfilling. Do you know that everyone can have a completely satisfactory marriage if they know how? Do you know that you have the right to a happy, fulfilling life?

Did you ever wonder why some people just are not able to achieve any measure of success in their work? They hate their work . . . don't understand what is expected . . . are always out of tune with the boss, etc. Yet others seem to do the right thing in the right way at the right time. These others like their work . . . understand what is expected . . . and are always in tune with the boss, etc. Do you realize that everyone can have work that they like and can be successful at? Do you realize you have the right to enjoyment and success in your work?

Did you ever wonder why some people are always sick? If something is going around, they get it. If they are in a car accident involving multiple persons, they are the only one injured, or the most seriously injured. Yet others rarely, or never, get sick. These others are the ones who walk away from accidents uninjured, or do not even have accidents. Do you realize that no one **has** to get sick or injured? Do you know that you have the right to be healthy and free of pain?

Did you ever wonder why some people are always out of step with what is happening? They are in the wrong place at the wrong time. They get on the down elevator when they need to go to the top floor. Yet others always seem to lead a charmed life, flowing in and out of situations in the right place, at the right time. If these people inadvertently get on the down elevator, you can bet they will find a twenty dollar bill at the bottom. Do you realize that it is entirely by your own choices that you are either "in tune" or "out of tune"? Did you know that you can program yourself to always be "in tune"? Did you know you have the right to be "in tune"?

Did you ever wonder why a few, selected people have paranormal experiences? They can tune in to other minds. They can obtain information from some mystical source. They can interact intelligently with people who are deceased. They can do things that are often considered miraculous. Yet others seem unable to walk and chew gum at the same time, let alone engage in paranormal experiences. Do you know that you have the innate ability to have these paranormal experiences? Do you know that you have the right to experience the so-called psychic world?

Well, you do have the innate ability to experience all of these things and even much more. You also have the right ... you do not need someone's permission ... you have a birthright to experience happiness, achievement, knowledge, fulfillment, and so forth.

People who do not experience all this enrichment simply haven't learned how. They keep trying to swim upstream against the current instead of learning how to flow with and utilize the natural energy patterns that are part of their being. They don't know that they have the right and the ability, so they relinquish their right and ability, and experience unhappiness instead.

There is one other important factor—responsibility. When you have a right, it can only be realized if you accept your responsibility for the right and exercise your responsibility to experience it. Having a right is meaningless unless you step up to your responsibility to claim the right.

This book will point out your rights and show you how to develop and use your innate abilities to realize those rights. But the responsibility is yours; it is your choice to do or not to do.

So we will be dealing with rights, innate ability, responsibility, and choices. And all of these in relation to experiences that are beyond hypnosis.

Hypnosis is often thought of as being the ultimate achievement in the use of the mind to solve problems or achieve goals. A smoker undergoes hypnosis and stops smoking. A person is hypnotized and doesn't feel the pain of surgery. A "loser" is hypnotized and becomes a "winner." What could possibly upstage such spectacular events as this? Well, hypnosis certainly is a marvelous, powerful tool. I am a clinical hypnotist, and I believe in the tremendous benefit that can be gained through hypnosis. However, I believe that hypnosis is just the beginning, and not the ultimate. Going beyond hypnosis offers experiences and achievement that dazzle the mind. As the late Al Jolson used to say, "You ain't seen nothin' yet!"

Your Skyscra,

A skyscraper is a very tall b
cement, and glass. It has a basement a
is something different on each floor, ai
that can quickly transport you to whicl.
to visit.

Your mind is similar to the skyscra, ...e-
ment and many floors. Each floor is a ɑ ... level of
conscious awareness, knowledge, and ability. Your mind is
made of pure, intelligent energy rather than of steel, cement,
and glass. Your elevator is your developed ability to go to
any level of mind you choose at will.

Imagine with me now for a few moments. Imagine you
are standing in front of an infinitely tall skyscraper that rep-
resents your mind. Look up and you are unable to see the
top because it disappears into the clouds and beyond. You
know your mind is endless just as is this skyscraper.

Now walk into the ground floor and look around.
There are many office doors. One is labeled *Self Preservation*.
Another is labeled *Food*, another *Shelter*, another *Safety*,
another *Procreation*. As you look at all the doors you realize
that this ground floor of your mind is concerned with the
basic necessities of life and survival. You are very familiar
with this floor (level). Over there are two elevator doors
side by side. One is labeled *Down Only*, and the other *Up
Only*. Walk over to the elevator marked *Down Only* and walk
into the elevator. Allow the elevator to descend to the basement. Allow the door to open, but do not leave the elevator.
Just peer through the door. You see a door labeled *Greed*,
another *Violence*, another *Hatred*, another *Pride*. There are
many more doors you can see with equally undesirable
labels. You realize that this is your own lower self. You realize that you have been to this level many times in the past,
and you are all too familiar with this level. You do not like it
here. You can feel the negative vibrations, and you vow to

return.

Now close the elevator door and lock the entrance to this basement level. Drop the key down the crack between the elevator and the elevator shaft. The key immediately falls down the shaft where you are not able to retrieve it.

Allow your elevator to return to your ground floor now. Exit the elevator. Turn around and close the door and place a large, powerful, unbreakable lock on the door. You will not use this *Down* elevator again.

Now enter your *Up* elevator and allow it to go to your first floor (level). Open the unlocked door and walk down the hallway and observe the doors on this first level. One is labeled *Dreams*, another *Hunches*. The labeled doors you are familiar with. You have been here before. There are many unlabeled doors also; you have not yet experienced what is behind these doors.

Now return to the elevator and go up to the second level. The door here is locked, and you are unable to see what is on this level. You determine in your mind to find a key for the lock so you will one day be able to open the door.

Return now to your ground floor. You have a greater awareness now of yourself. You know you have a sub-nature which you do not ever again wish to experience. You know you have some awareness of a higher self. You also know that you have hundreds of levels of higher self that you have not yet unlocked. You vow to find a way to unlock those higher levels and experience them.

Walk outside and gaze upward once again at the skyscraper of your mind, noting how immeasurably tall it is. You have had but a mini-excursion into your mind. You want more.

In Chapter 5, we will make extensive use of your skyscraper and elevator. You will learn to unlock and experience all levels of your higher self at will.

As you go increasingly higher and higher in your sky-scraper you will encounter increasingly sophisticated and esoteric experiences. At some level, you will satiate all conscious experiences; the next level begins the subconscious. At some higher level of awareness you encounter the super-conscious, etc. The only limit on your achievement is the limit you place on it. If you don't want to go beyond the twentieth floor, you won't. The very top floor is total enlightenment, fulfillment, knowledge, and realization.

Getting There

To achieve the higher levels of mind, you must learn to lower your brain operating frequency to the point where you can transport yourself to the necessary level. The 30-session program explained in a later chapter will train you to do this.

Your brain frequency fluctuates countless times every day, spontaneously, as the need arises.

The most notable time that we can all identify is when we go to sleep at night. You lay your head on the pillow, close your eyes, and your brain automatically starts cycling down so you can rest, dream, and become rejuvenated. The sleep process is necessary for us to maintain our mental and physical health and balance.

Beta. When we are awake and performing our daily chores, our brain operates in the beta frequency range. This is from about 14 cycles per second on up, with most of our activity being at about 20 to 22 cycles per second. This is our conscious mind. At this level, we reason, rationalize, and execute whatever chores we need to do. If your brain frequency gets too high, say around 60 cycles per second, you would be in acute hysteria. Much higher than that would probably bring disastrous results, perhaps death.

Alpha. Between about 7 and 14 cycles per second is the

alpha range of brain activity. Here is where daydreaming and nocturnal dreaming take place. Hypnosis also takes place here.

Theta. Between 4 and 7 cycles per second is the theta state. All our emotional experiences are recorded here. This also is the range from which you can launch into psychic experience.

Delta. Frequencies less than 4 cycles per second are encountered in total unconsciousness, the delta state.

Sleep Cycle. When you drift into sleep, your brain quickly cycles out of beta, through alpha and theta rather quickly, and into delta for a short while. Typically, you might make the transition from beta into delta in about 30 minutes, then remain in delta for from 30 to 90 minutes. At that point, your brain would cycle up into theta, and into alpha where you would dream for a while, then cycle back down into theta, then up into alpha for more dreaming. In an eight-hour sleep period, you might spend 30 to 90 minutes in delta, 30 to 60 in theta, and the rest of the time in alpha.

This is an illustrative sleep cycle. It will vary from person to person, and even from night to night with the same person.

The important thing to note is that altered states are a natural phenomena that you go through every day.

Even when you are awake, you will dip into alpha and theta frequently for very brief periods. For instance, you hit your finger with the hammer while pounding a nail. Your brain dips into theta to record the pain. Or perhaps you are studying and trying to memorize some material. You look off into space to record the material in your brain at alpha.

Achieving Altered States. Quite simply, all you need to do to become a psychic is to learn how to deliberately cause your brain to go into theta and remain there for as long as you wish without your falling asleep. Easy to say, but it takes some effort and discipline to do. Also, there is a bit more to becoming a psychic than this. All will be covered before the end of the book.

Visualization. The key to achieving theta at will and then using that state to achieve psychic experiences is visualization. A short while ago, I had you take a visual excursion of your skyscraper mind. We will be concerned a great deal with visualizing.

The Gunfighter. To become a good practicing psychic you are going to become a gunfighter with your mind.

In the old West, the gunfighter practiced incessantly until his eyes, instincts, hands, and gun became as one. He got to the point where he did not think at all. He was a finely tuned machine that acted with precision and accuracy faster than he would have time to think about it.

So, too, must you do this with your mind. You can get to the point where you alter your state of mind as fast as the gunfighter's draw. You will lock into the necessary level of your mind as accurately as the gunman's aim. When you become totally at one with yourself, you will be a master. Do not expect to be a master after reading this book. Becoming a master is a lifelong pursuit—perhaps many lifetimes.

This book will provide the precision gun, teach you to draw and shoot, and help you hone your senses to keen awareness. But the practice is entirely up to you. If you wish to become a mental gunfighter, you must practice, practice, and practice every day. And the mechanism of practice is visualization.

The Mind. The most difficult thing for most people to comprehend is just what the mind is. The most common misconception is that the mind and the brain are the same thing. Not so.

The brain is a physical collection of flesh, nerves, chemicals, blood, and cells that is housed in our skull. The brain is like a super computer. It can remember, reason, and perform all sorts of mental wizardry. When our container, our physical body, dies, the brain also dies.

The mind is the total energy that is us. While we are housed in our physical container, the mind uses our brain. The mind is nonphysical; it belongs to the spiritual or psychic world, and it never dies. The mind is who we are.

CHAPTER 4

PSYCHIC EXPERIENCES

In the previous chapters I discussed psychic experiences in a general way. In Chapter 5 you will learn how to become a psychic. But what exactly is a psychic experience?

Psychic experience embraces a wide range of paranormal activities. To mention a few: telepathic communication; out-of-body travel; psychic healing; communication with nonphysical entities (some people say ghosts, but I prefer entities or discarnates). These are only a few. Categorizing or naming them is not particularly important. The important thing is to understand the nature of the psychic world and how to utilize it effectively for benefit.

Have you ever had a strong hunch that you should or should not do something? If you follow the hunch, you are glad because it was beneficial information. If you rationalize that the hunch didn't make sense and you go against it, you end up regretting that decision. This is a valid psychic experience. Your higher mind was furnishing you information for your benefit. Whether you follow it or not is your choice. Generally, if you habitually ignore your hunches, your higher mind will stop giving them to you because you haven't shown appreciation. Then you are on your own because you have cut off a valuable information source. Of course, you can re-establish that communication path by completing the 30-session program described in Chapter 5. If you habitually follow your hunches, your higher mind will give you more and more guidance because you have shown appreciation.

Has a phone call ever come from a person who you were preparing to call at that same moment? This is a valid psychic experience of mental telepathic communication between two minds. Remember—there is no such thing as coincidence.

Have you ever had an experience that you felt you had had before even though you knew you hadn't? This is called *déjà vu* and is a valid psychic experience. The experience can be due to either of the following:

1. You had the same or a similar experience in a previous lifetime. All lifetime experiences are in the mind and available to you. Encountering a similar experience in this lifetime can invoke the memory of a previous lifetime experience.

2. Your mind had looked ahead in time to the experience and recorded it. Then when you actually encounter the experience, it seems like a replay.

The experiences I have just described are quite common, and the chances are that you have had several of them.

In order to give you an even broader and more specific description of psychic experiences, I devote this chapter to a sampling of some of those I have had. My experiences are not all encompassing, but they should give you a good idea of what the psychic world is all about.

Each person has his/her own kind of experience. One may "hear" information. Another may get a "feeling" or "awareness." Another is good at sending mental messages; another at receiving. One person may have excellent communication with entities. Some may experience a wide variety of experiences; others only a few. Do not be discouraged if you do not experience everything. You are a special channel, and you will function in accordance with your innate specialty. Be pleased with what you get and who you are.

In an earlier chapter I mentioned that esoteric and practical experiences could be blended for a beneficial result. In some of the personal experiences I am about to relate, you will see how I used information gained through psychic means to bring about a practical "Earthly" result.

My First Awakening Experience

I had two profound, spontaneous psychic experiences within a couple weeks of each other that altered my life forever. The first occurred about two months before the United States lifted the restriction of gold prices (held to about $35 an ounce) and allowed the gold price to float and seek its own level. To the best of my recollection, this was in the very early 1970s.

I was the publications manager for a large computer equipment engineering/manufacturing company and had forty-seven people reporting to me. The psychic world was not of any particular interest to me.

One Monday, one of my employees (I'll call him Harry) came into my office to talk about some job-related problem. I was sitting at my desk doing some paperwork. When I looked up to greet him, I had an instantaneous experience unlike anything I had ever had.

It was as though a movie projector in the back of my head projected a movie on the inside of my forehead. The movie showed Harry attempting suicide the previous day by swallowing a quantity of pills. I saw him lapse into unconsciousness. Then his wife (I'll call her Rose), who was a registered nurse, found him and had him rushed to the hospital where his stomach was pumped. Rose was on the hospital staff, and she was able to stifle any news reports about it. Harry came to work the next day so there wouldn't be any suspicions raised. I saw this whole thing in my head in just a few seconds.

I was so startled that I sat there dumbfounded for a short while just staring into space and thinking about it.

Finally, I realized that Harry had been talking to me, and I didn't know what he had been saying.

"I'm sorry, Harry," I muttered, "I am preoccupied. Would you repeat that?"

Harry started to talk, and that movie went off in my head again, giving me an instant replay.

I didn't understand what was happening, but it was too real and vivid for me to ignore. I got up and walked to the door and closed it. Then I pulled up a chair next to Harry.

"Harry, do you have a personal problem that we need to talk about?" I asked.

"No! No! Everything is fine," he said. His sudden visible nervousness told me he was lying.

Then my movie played again. I decided to throw caution to the wind and ask Harry point blank.

"Did you try to take your own life yesterday?" I asked.

Harry grew pale and began to weep. I let him get it out of his system.

"How did you know?" he finally managed to say. "Rose called you, didn't she?"

"No, Rose didn't call me. How I know is not important. What is important is . . . " I was interrupted in midsentence by another movie.

This movie showed Harry using a gun to execute a successful attempt the following Sunday. He had a plan that would not be thwarted.

I finished my interrupted sentence, " . . . is that you do not go through with your plan next Sunday."

"My God! How could you possibly know?" He began shaking and weeping again.

When he gained composure, I began to speak words that were being channeled through me. I could feel the intelligence coming into the crown of my head. I seemed to process the intelligence and speak the words.

"Harry, I know you are feeling a lot of pain, and you want to die. It is your life, and you can choose to die if you want to. You have that right. But you also have another right. That is the right to live, and you have never explored this right. I will make a commitment to you if you will make one to me. Give me two weeks of your life. Do not kill yourself for two weeks. During that time, let me get you on a medical program. Also, I want you to come to my office every afternoon from one until three and we will talk. If you still want to kill yourself after the two weeks are up, go ahead. I promise not to alert anyone or try to stop you. I am not asking much. You have had this pain for forty years. You can bear it for just two more weeks."

"You won't tell?"

"I promise."

"OK. I'll give it two weeks," he said.

I immediately took Harry to the company doctor who got him started on a therapy program.

When I returned to my office, I wondered what in the world I was going to talk to Harry about when he started coming in for daily chats. Everything I had said to Harry was just a parroting of words I was fed from some intelligence source that I didn't understand. I certainly wasn't equipped by knowledge or training to handle this kind of situation.

However, my apprehension was put to rest when Harry came in to see me each day. As soon as he closed the door and sat down, my unseen intelligence source provided me with the words. I could feel them enter the crown of my head. Harry and I learned together.

After two weeks, Harry came in to tell me his decision.

"Bill," he said, "I am not out of the woods yet. I still have a long way to go. But the furthest thing from my mind is suicide. I want to live. Thank you for helping me explore my right to live."

Epilogue: Harry is still alive and happy today. He raised his children to adulthood, and has found meaning in life. All this because I allowed myself to function as an open psychic channel from my higher intelligence.

At the time, of course, I didn't know that was what I was doing. I had no idea of what was going on. After pondering it for a week or so, I dismissed it as some sort of unexplainable fluke. Little did I know.

But my higher mind wasn't finished with me, as indicated by my second awakening experience.

My Second Awakening Experience

Several weeks after my experience with Harry was over, I was alone in my office tending to the ever-present paperwork. Harry was no longer in my conscious thoughts.

Someone said, "Sell all your stock now." It was said softly but with authority.

I looked around to see who had entered my office. No one was there. I shrugged it off, and went back to my work.

"Sell all your stock now!" This time the voice was louder and closer.

Again, no one was there. I got up and looked into the hallway. No one was there either.

I sat and pondered the words for a few moments. I reasoned that selling the stock was foolish. I had purchased shares of my company's stock through payroll deduction for close to eighteen years. The stock was now nearly four hundred dollars a share and was considered to be the strongest and most valuable stock on the market. Again, I returned to my paperwork.

"Sell all your stock now!" Now it was a command.

"No!" I mentally retorted.

"I was right about Harry wasn't I?" the voice boomed.

The hair on the back of my neck bristled. Without hesitation, I picked up the phone and dialed a friend who was a stockbroker.

"Don, sell all my stock now."

Don tried for twenty minutes to talk me out of it. It didn't make sense to sell that stock. It was just going to keep going up.

I stuck to my guns, and he finally said, "OK, Bill, I will place a sell order. But you tell your wife I was against it. I don't want her raising hell with me."

"Now," he continued, "what do you want me to do with the money?"

The voice said, "Reinvest it." So I repeated to Don, "Reinvest it."

"In what?" Don asked.

I paused to wait for the voice to tell me in what, but there was no voice. I felt foolish. I didn't know anything about the stock market.

To keep from appearing to be a complete idiot, I said, "Talk to me about some issues."

Don started talking about issues, but none of it made any sense to me. Then he casually mentioned one issue, which I had never heard of, and the voice said, "Buy that."

"Reinvest all the money in that," I said.

"Bill, you are out of your mind. That is a volatile high-risk issue. You could lose everything in the twinkling of an eye." He spent another twenty minutes trying to dissuade me.

Finally, he relented and placed a buy order. The stock was in South African gold mines.

Epilogue: Two days later the bottom dropped out of

the stock I had sold for nearly four hundred dollars a share. It plummeted to one hundred ninety a share in one day. I had sold at a high. It was several years before that stock fully recovered.

A few days after that, the U.S. government lifted the price freeze on gold, and it quickly began to climb. My gold stock soared, split three for one, and soared some more.

A little over six months later, while at my desk, the voice said, "Sell." Without hesitation, I sold and made a handsome profit.

Then, unpredictably, I was forced out of the company after eighteen years of service by a series of reorganizations and politics.

My profit from the stock enabled me to live the next four years while I traveled, studied, became a clinical hypnotist, became a professional astrologer, honed my psychic abilities, engaged in giving psychic readings, and started on the path to becoming a successful author and lecturer. Thus, my life was totally redirected by my higher mind. Every step of the way since then I have had psychic guidance and have had the most incredible experiences. In this book, I share a few of these experiences with you to help you learn. But this book is only the tip of the iceberg.

The Locomotive

Not all psychic experiences are so profound as those I have just described. Many are just strong feelings or hunches about something.

About twenty years ago, my wife and our three young children and I lived in a small town in upstate New York. The activities of the town centered around the local VFW, which was very active. The VFW had purchased an old steam locomotive and refurbished it to use in parades. They put in a gasoline engine, outfitted it with heavy-duty truck tires, and remodeled the coal tender with seats for passengers. The official driver was a friend I'll call Nelson.

Nelson pulled up in the locomotive in the street in front of our house one day. On board where his wife and another couple we knew casually. He wanted us to come aboard and go for a joy ride. My wife and children were ecstatic as I helped them board.

Then just as I started to step up into the tender, a powerful feeling of apprehension gripped me. I knew there was going to be an accident.

I quickly stepped back to the ground. My wife and children refused to get off. Everyone jeered about how I was a "party pooper." They drove off.

By the time I got my car out of the garage, the locomotive had disappeared over a hill. I followed.

At the first curve after topping the hill, I caught up with them. The locomotive was in a ditch after first sheering off a telephone pole. The woman who was sitting next to my wife was bleeding profusely from the head. Apparently a piece of the damaged telephone pole had hit her. Thankfully, no one else was hurt.

I took the woman for medical attention and transported everyone else to her house for an impromptu party. The woman's cut was not serious, and she also joined the party. All in all, it wasn't a serious matter.

Then why did I get the psychic warning? Probably to protect me. It is likely that I would have been sitting next to my wife instead of the woman if I had boarded the locomotive. Hence, it is likely that I would have been injured.

When I reflect over my life, I can count dozens of times when I was protected either by a psychic experience or by a freak set of circumstances. I won't belabor all of them with you. This one incident describes quite well a subtle kind of psychic experience for benefit. My higher mind seems to do an excellent job of taking care of me. It will for you, too, if you allow it.

Takra

Takra was my youngest daughter's beautiful Samoyed dog. Takra had become seriously ill with an anal infection which defied the veterinarian's best efforts to clear up.

The doctor finally said that it was too serious a matter to continue to try to treat with medication because the dog just was not responding at all. Takra, usually an energetic animal, just lay listlessly and in some discomfort. He wouldn't eat or drink. The doctor said surgery was necessary, and it needed to be done soon.

My daughter said, "No!" She feared the dog would die from the anesthesia. Also she didn't want him cut open. She was hoping for a miracle.

She came to me sobbing, "Daddy, can't you help Takra? I have seen you help people. Why not a dog?"

"I'll give it my best shot," I promised. I sat down cross-legged in the middle of the floor and altered my consciousness into the theta region. Then I sought the level where I have my own psychic workshop.

I mentally commanded the image of Takra into my psychic workshop. With my intelligence, I scanned his entire body internally and externally and corrected all the abnormalities I detected. The anal region was a mass of pus, infection, blood, and redness.

In my psychic workshop, I have everything I need to correct any problem. To get rid of the pus, I inserted a powerful suction tube similar to that used by dentists. I drew out all the pus. I scraped all the infection off with steel wool and cleansed the area with a powerful medicine labeled "cure-all" from my psychic medicine chest. I processed all his blood through a purifying machine and filled him with the cleansed blood. I sprayed the area with a color restorer so everything looked normal and healthy. Then I took a needle labeled "strength and energy" and gave him an injection. Satisfied that Takra was restored to health and balance, I brought myself out of theta and opened my eyes.

My daughter went immediately to the room where Takra had been lying. She found him standing and stretching as though awakening from a long nap. He pounced at her, wanting to play. She examined him externally. There was no seepage, no swelling, no discoloration. He looked and acted fine.

The next day she took him to the vet where he was given a clean bill of health.

"The medicine must have had a long-delayed action," the vet had said. "I've never seen anything like that before, but what else could it have been?"

What else, indeed?

The kinds of things I've described here are things you can learn to do by completing the 30-session program in Chapter 5. Notice in psychic healing that you do symbolically whatever is natural for you to do to correct the problem.

For instance, you might perceive a defective liver as having yellow spots on it. So you sand off the spots with a power sander and paint the liver to restore its natural color. Or you might treat blood cancer by having millions of cancer-eating piranha swimming in the bloodstream, devouring the cancer cells. A blocked intestine might be cleared by using a roto-rooter. A damaged nerve could be replaced by a fine, sensitive wire. And so forth. It is your powerful imagination and visualization while in theta that makes the psychic power work. You visualize a roto-rooter cleaning out a blockage, but your mind and the recipient's mind translate that into natural healing action.

Dad's Shell Hole

My father spent eighteen months in the front lines in World War I. Here is a psychic experience he had while in battle.

Dad and eight comrades were huddled in the protection of a huge shell hole to protect them from the blistering machine-gun fire that saturated the air above their heads.

Dad said he suddenly became uneasy in the shell hole. He had an irresistible urge to get out of there even though it didn't make any logical sense.

"Don't do it, Shorty," his companions advised. "You will be killed." Dad said some unseen force drove him to crawl out of the hole on his stomach. He knew bullets were but inches above him. He crawled about a hundred yards to the stump of what was once a large tree and sat behind it for shelter from the enemy gunfire.

Then he turned and gazed back to where he had come from just as an artillery shell exploded in that old shell hole. All his comrades were killed.

Dad had listened to his higher mind, and was saved from death.

Encounter With A Ghost

I have had several encounters with entities or discarnates (commonly called ghosts) over the years. I'll relate just one case that I found most interesting. This is the only case in this book in which I have altered some of the facts. I have done so to protect the privacy and feelings of those who are still living who were involved in some way in this situation. The actual psychic encounter was exactly as I have it written here. What I have altered are the physical environment and circumstances to disguise where and when the situation took place.

A friend of mine who lived in another state had a string of franchised bookstores. These were small bookstores that were usually run by the franchisee and one part-time employee. Such was the case of one of those franchises near my home. The owner/operator was an attractive lady in her thirties who I'll call Lisa. She had one part-time employee, a lady also in her thirties who I'll call Fern. Both ladies loved the business. It was Lisa's whole life, and they had a profitable operation in excess of what might be expected for such a small bookstore. Their love, devotion, and hard work were apparently infectious because people liked to trade there.

Then one Saturday, Lisa was killed in a tragic accident enroute to open up the bookstore. Fern went into depression and couldn't bear to ever enter the store again.

My friend flew to town to take care of handling the legal matters involved with the death of the franchisee. He was in a bind. He needed someone reliable to immediately take over the store on a temporary basis until a new buyer could be found and legal matters straightened out.

He asked my wife and me to manage and operate the store. He offered an attractive salary to each of us. Fortunately, I had just finished a writing contract the week before and was available. We said OK, but only for a few months until he found a new buyer. He gave us the keys, and the next day we opened up the store, and also opened up one of the most interesting experiences of our life.

The street door opened into the bookstore itself. At the far end of the store was a door that opened into a small office containing a desk and chair, telephone, five-drawer file cabinet, and two vinyl-covered recliner chairs. The corners were stacked with boxes of books.

The first week was just very busy. We had to learn the business and inventory. Lisa's friends and clientele called or came in to inquire about her death, the funeral arrangements, etc. I audited the financial status. We quickly learned why there were two recliner chairs in the office; the hours were long and active, and once in a while we needed to rest.

Lisa's estranged husband came in to claim some personal items that were not part of the business. He seemed like a nice person, but he certainly showed no remorse over Lisa's death. Even though he and Lisa had been separated for quite a few months, I thought he might have shown some feeling.

On Monday morning of the second week we found a surprise waiting for us. All the drawers of the five-drawer file cabinet were open, and the contents were removed and scattered all over the floor. As far as we could tell, nothing was missing. Since we had the only key, and there were no signs of forced entry, we were perplexed.

The next day, books had been removed from the shelves and scattered.

The day after, my wife Dee and I were eating lunch in the office when we heard the outside door open and close. Dee walked out to greet the expected customer, but no one was there. Again, some books were pulled from the shelf.

The following day was a repeat of the previous day. This time I ran out to the sidewalk to see who the prankster was. No one was there.

This kind of activity persisted off and on for several months. Dee said she was sure someone unseen was constantly watching her; she could feel it.

One day I noticed that the desk had a pullout type of writing board. I pulled it out for no particular reason and was stunned by what was taped to it. There were photographs of Lisa and Fern in embraces that disclosed that they were lovers. There also were love poems from each to the other which were quite sexually explicit. This explained Lisa's estrangement from her husband, his coolness toward her death, and Fern's depression over Lisa's death. I wondered if this was what our unseen visitor had been looking for.

From that moment on, we had no more visits from our unseen visitor until the day my friend phoned to tell me that effective the first of next month he had a new buyer for the bookstore. The owner was a woman named Maggie Johnson.

The next day I was resting on one of the recliners with my eyes closed. I had gone to theta for deep relaxation. Dee was out front minding the store.

I heard the vinyl of the adjacent recliner squeak as though someone was sitting down on it. I knew no one had entered the room, so I mentally asked, "Who is there?"

"Lisa," was the mental reply I received.

"Why? What do you want?"

"I want you out of my bookstore."

"Why?"

"Because you are a man."

"Haven't I been doing a good job?" I asked.

"Yes. You have done an excellent job managing for me, but you are a man and I want you out!"

"I will be leaving the end of the month for sure," I mentally replied. "Is that all right?"

"Fine. Who is taking your place?"

"The franchise has been purchased by a woman named Maggie Johnson."

"Maggie Johnson! I will not have that woman in my bookstore. She is incompetent!"

"Lisa," I said, "you are dead. You have no purpose here now. Leave and find peace."

"I will not leave! This is my bookstore. If Maggie Johnson takes over, I will see this place bankrupt in six months."

Then Lisa left, and I never personally encountered her again. But the story isn't over.

I phoned my friend and told him of the encounter with Lisa. He and a professional psychic came to the store. They both felt a powerful negative presence. Their attempt to exorcise Lisa from the premises was unsuccessful.

In the remaining days I had there, business just stopped. I had only thirty-five dollars in sales in a week.

Then Maggie Johnson took over her franchise. No one came into the store. She hung on for six months and had to declare bankruptcy.

Out Of Body

Some people are able to leave their body and travel to distant places and bring back information gained from that excursion. They can do this while awake and conscious; they do it at will. Some others do it spontaneously; that is, they have not learned to control it. It just happens without warning.

Most are like me, they have an occasional out-of-body excursion while asleep and then later awaken with a recollection of it. I have not yet learned how to do it while awake, so I am not able to teach you how. What I do is project mentally to where I want to be, and that is what I teach in this book.

I did have one unusual out-of-body encounter that I will share with you.

One of my early psychic teachers was a very pretty young woman named Marcia. She was a natural psychic and had been doing out-of-body travel at will for as long as she could remember. She was in her teens before she realized that she was unusual . . . that she was not like everyone.

Marcia was conducting a series of lectures and training sessions. I was one of ten students in her class.

She had taught us how to reach theta, and we were all in that state, eyes closed, while she talked to us from the front of the room.

I heard her voice move to the side of the room and then down to where I was seated. Then, in an instant, her voice was inside my head, and my entire body felt bloated. After about fifteen seconds, her voice moved to the front of the room, and I no longer felt bloated.

She talked us up from theta and had us open our eyes.

"Did anyone have any unusual experiences in theta?" she asked.

No hands went up. I knew I should have raised my hand, but I thought I was being foolish.

"Yes. One person did have an unusual experience." Marcia continued. "Will you tell us about it, Bill?"

"So it wasn't my imagination," I said. Then I related my experience.

Marcia smiled. She said she had gone out of body and walked over (while her physical body remained in the front of the room) and sat down inside my body for a short while.

Healing Hands

Of all my psychic experiences, this one stands out in my mind as the most extraordinary.

My wife Dee works part time as a food demonstrator for food brokers. On one occasion while working, she met a woman I'll call Nancy whose husband had been told by his doctor that day that he had only two months to live. It seems the husband (I'll call him Tom) had an infection in his intestine that was literally poisoning him to death; it was untreatable. The infected section of intestine could be removed by surgery, but Tom's physical condition was so debilitated that the doctor said he would surely die on the operating table. Life-saving surgery would kill him, and yet he would die without the surgery. Some choice!

Dee was so moved by Nancy's story that she came home that night and asked, "Bill, why don't you help that man?"

"What can I do? If the doctor says there is no hope, I don't see how I can improve matters."

"I've seen you help people. You have a way of just talking to people and making them feel better. Just call Nancy up and ask her and Tom to come over tonight. I have her number."

Dee handed me a slip of paper with a phone number on it.

"I don't know these people," I said. "I don't know what to do."

"Just call. You will think of something to say."

I never could refuse my wife anything, so I called and invited Nancy and Tom over. As an aside, I found out later that my wife had told Nancy that I was going to call and ask them over. That explained why they were ready and appeared at our house less than thirty minutes later.

Tom's physical appearance was appalling. His six-foot frame weighed less than a hundred pounds. There was no fleshiness at all . . . just pale skin tautly stretched over bone. His eyes looked hollow and dead, and he didn't walk . . . he just shuffled along on feet too heavy for his emaciated legs to lift. His shoulders drooped. Both arms were a mass of seeping scabs from the dozens of needles he had received. He didn't even have enough healing power to heal the puncture wound of an injection. I could easily see why the doctor said that Tom would die on the operating table. The thought crossed my mind that I had seen healthier-looking cadavers.

The four of us settled in the living room to talk. Dee served tea.

I had no idea what to do or say. I had a vague notion that maybe I could hynotize him, but then what?

The hypnosis thought flew right out the window as soon as I started to talk to him. He was sixty-five-percent deaf in both ears. When I sat directly in front of him and shouted slowly, he got about every third or fourth word. Now what? I didn't know how to hypnotize someone who couldn't hear me, and I sure couldn't do it by writing notes.

So I did what I always do when I don't know what to do. I leaned back, relaxed, and went into theta. I mentally uttered one word to my higher mind . . . "Help!"

And help came thundering into my conscious awareness instantly. I received complete instructions as to what I should do. Frankly, what I was told to do didn't make any sense to me at all, but I had learned long ago not to question the instructions I receive from my higher mind. Just do it. Here is what I was told to do, and did indeed implement.

I led Tom into an adjacent room where we had a recliner chair and motioned for him to sit down. On a paper I wrote him a note that said, "Lean the recliner back and relax. Close your eyes and do not open them until I touch your forehead." He complied. Then I took my hands and placed them on each side of his head about a half-inch away from actually touching him. I began to slowly move my hands downward to begin scanning his entire body. Almost instantly my hands grew hot, as though immersed in hot water. The longer I scanned, the hotter my hands became; they physically became quite red and puffy. I scanned him with my hands for about ten minutes. Then my hands suddenly cooled off and returned to normal color. I knew I was finished, so I touched his forehead to signal him to open his eyes.

Tom bolted from the chair. "My God, what did you do? I felt on fire, but it didn't hurt. I feel great."

His skin had turned to a normal pink hue. His eyes sparkled. And when we walked back to join our wives, he walked briskly.

The rest of the evening he talked nonstop. And when we addressed him in our normal speaking voice, he heard every word.

Dee prepared a snack, and he devoured it lustily. His wife said he had not eaten solid food in many days.

Over the next several weeks he improved so much that

the doctor said he could now survive surgery. The surgery was successful.

I visited Tom in the hospital after surgery. His arms were still full of seeping scabs. Apparently all his healing power had been directed where it was most needed, and the scabs were untreated.

"Bill, can't you do something about these?" Tom asked me, indicating the scabs.

I repeated the same procedure I had used on him several weeks previously.

The next morning Tom phoned to tell me that all the scabs had fallen off during the night, and he was completely healed where the scabs had been.

He was discharged from the hospital a week earlier than the doctor had anticipated.

For the next several weeks I worked with Tom both in person and on the phone. He had the most negative attitude and poorest self-image of any person I had ever met. I told him this was at the root of his problems. I helped him learn self-hypnosis and trained him to restructure himself mentally. Then I put him on his own with the advice that he had to assume responsibility for his own life. He could not live through me, and I couldn't be available day and night to do it for him. I told him that if he returned to his negativism, he would also return to ill health.

At no time did I charge him a penny, nor did he ever offer any. I felt, and still do, that this was a responsibility and an opportunity for me to serve and learn. At no time did he ever say, "Thank you." His wife did thank me though. She said that, to her knowledge, Tom had never said "Thank you" in his entire life.

For several years Tom practiced off and on what I had taught him and stayed in reasonably good shape. But he allowed himself to eventually slip back into his old negative thought patterns. He stopped trying to help himself. He made life miserable for himself, his wife, and anyone else he came in contact with.

When I found out, Tom was already at death's door again. This time he had given up; he apparently wanted to die. Nothing could be done. He died, but he had gained about five extra years of life and had been given the opportunity to learn and grow spiritually. It is unfortunate that he chose to not learn and grow, but he will get the opportunity again sometime, somewhere.

We all get the opportunity to learn, grow, and experience everything necessary for total self-realization. And we get to do it again and again and again, as long as necessary, until we get it right.

How much better it is if we do it right the first time. Let's make that choice now, and then do it so we can get on to bigger and better things.

Career Path Change
Every day there are literally dozens of ways to use your psychic ability in small, practical ways to help yourself or others.

Here is just one example.

My youngest daughter, Eileen, was in her final year of high school and planned to go to college. All her high school courses were business courses, and her part-time job was as a secretary/bookkeeper. For several years, her announced plan was to get a degree in business administration.

One day she seemed troubled and confused. I asked what the problem was, and she said she didn't know.

"Then let's find out," I said. I sat down cross-legged on the floor right then and there and went into theta and did a psychic reading on her.

The information came to me quickly.

"You really don't want a business career," I said. "You

recognize it as a good bread and butter occupation, but you find it empty of fulfillment and challenge."

"That's true," she responded.

"Your strongest innate asset is your ability to teach children, especially the very young children, and you have a great love of children."

"I've never thought about that," she said. "I don't think teaching appeals to me, but I do like the stimulation of small children."

"I am just telling you what your natural abilities are as I read them. Think about it, but don't do it because I say so. Make your own choice in your own time."

Then I came out of theta. The reading was over.

Eileen started reading literature about teaching and talking to teachers about teaching as a career. Something deep inside her caught fire, and she became excited.

She got her degree in early childhood education and is certified to teach the "little ones," preschool, kindergarten, and grades one and two. She is delighted with her career choice.

As you become a practicing psychic, look for these little daily opportunities to use your abilities. You will do yourself, others, and the world a lot of good, and you will keep your skills tuned up. If you want to become a virtuoso in the use of your mind, you must use it as often as you can. "Practice makes perfect" should become your guiding creed.

The Possessed Oriental

About ten o'clock one evening my phone rang. A very distraught man was on the other end of the line.

"You don't know me," he said, "but I have heard about you, and I need your help. I am going out of my mind and may kill myself, but I don't want to." He had what I thought was an Oriental accent.

"What is your name?" I asked.

"Johnny Kim."

"Where do you live?"

He gave me an address in one of the toughest, most undesirable parts of town.

We talked a while, and I became convinced that he did indeed have a serious problem that I might be able to help him with.

I told him I would be there in about a half-hour.

"You are crazy!" my wife said. "That part of town isn't safe in daylight let alone this time of night. You might be robbed or killed. You don't know that man. You don't owe him anything. What about me if you are killed? You owe me more than some strange voice on the telephone."

I understood her concern and fears. But I also understand the nature of life and of being involved. There is no such thing as not wanting to be involved. We are all born involved whether we want to be or not. Many choose to ignore that responsibility, but I do not choose to ignore it. But this was not the time to discuss the matter with her.

I clipped on my belt holster and slipped my .38 Smith & Wesson stubby into it.

"I will be fine, Hon. Please don't worry. I know what I'm doing."

Then I left to keep my appointment.

Kim's apartment was what once must have been the attic of a three-story house built around the turn of the century.

He ushered me into his main living area. It was about a twenty foot by twenty foot room completely devoid of furniture except for an old rocking chair in the center of the room. His wife sat in the chair rocking their infant child; both looked malnourished. A single, unshaded, low-wattage light bulb hung from the ceiling. She just nodded and smiled weakly when I said hello. Two blanket pallets that served as their beds were in a far corner. Some cardboard boxes lined one wall. I assume their few clothes and possessions were in the boxes.

A homemade partition somewhat separated the kitchen area from the living area, but I could see it quite clearly. It, too, had a single, unshaded low-wattage light bulb suspended from the ceiling. Their table was a dilapidated folding card table, and there were two straight-backed kitchen chairs that appeared to have come from a salvage sale. The stove was a two-burner hot plate. A vintage sink and a homemade cabinet rounded out the appointments.

I assume they had a toilet, but I don't know where it was.

Kim lit a kerosene lamp and led me into an adjoining space not much larger than a walk-in closet where we were to consult. He sat the lamp on the floor. There was not one article of any kind in the room. He fetched the two kitchen chairs for us to sit on.

Then began a strange case. In halting English, Kim poured out the essentials of his plight. It seems he worked as a parking lot attendant. His wage was much less than the legal minimum, but he didn't know that. He would have been eligible for welfare, which would have paid him more money, but his Oriental pride would not permit him to do so as long as he was capable of working. Desperate for money to provide food and bare survival necessities for his wife and child, he began skimming money from the daily receipts at the parking lot.

He only took what he absolutely needed, and in the week he had been doing it had only skimmed fifty dollars. But he was a very moral person, and his conscience troubled him greatly. He saw himself becoming an habitual thief. He worried about getting caught and being sent to jail. Then what would his wife and child do? And if he didn't continue to steal, how could he feed and care for his family?

These things were tearing him up inside until he was nearly crazy with fear and discouragement. He felt he needed to consult with someone. Kim was not religious, but he believed that talking to a clergyman might help him. Ordinarily this would have been a wise choice, and he would have gotten help. Unfortunately, Kim went to the nearest clergyman who happened to be out of balance himself. The clergyman ranted and raved at Kim . . . called him sinful and evil and said he was damned to hell now and always . . . and said he was possessed of the devil and there was no hope for him.

Kim returned home so emotionally shaken that he was planning to kill himself. He was absolutely convinced he was possessed of evil. Only the sight of his wife and child, whom he loved, made him determined to look elsewhere for help. He recalled seeing a small ad I had placed in the personal column of the newspaper, and he phoned me.

Clearly, there were two things I needed to do. First, rid him of his fear, and secondly, help him get financial support.

I altered my state to theta and did a psychic reading. I immediately encountered a powerful negative wall of fear that was difficult to penetrate. Next I directed my attention to the clergyman and told Kim what I found. In essence, the clergyman was an old man who was bitter about being sent to this rundown parish in which to spend his final years. He felt he deserved better recognition from his church. He also was somewhat mentally out of balance due partly to his failing health and partly to his negative attitude. He was an old-school traditionalist who saw everything as either black or white, and he saw evil everywhere. He also had a considerable amount of racial prejudice.

I sent the clergyman love, courage, and peace. Then I redirected my attention to Kim.

Kim's wall of fear was considerably less powerful now after hearing what I had just told him, and I was able to establish solid contact at a psychic level with him.

It was quickly apparent to me that he was a good person who was trying to do his best, but he didn't know how to go about it. He was very naive, uneducated, and socially unsophisticated. My higher mind also told me that Kim really did believe that he was possessed of evil.

In reality, he was not possessed at all, but he really believed he was. So my higher mind directed me to exorcise the evil from him so he would feel balanced and clean again.

I didn't know anything about exorcism, but my higher mind directed me through the procedure.

I am not including in this book the exorcism procedure I used. The reason is that this sort of thing can potentially get you into a lot of trouble; it also can be dangerous in some circumstances. It is not something you are likely to ever need, and I don't want you experimenting with this sort of thing. If you ever need to know about exorcism, I will leave it up to your own experience and your higher mind to direct you.

After the exorcism, Kim felt fine. He knew that there was nothing wrong with him now.

Then I talked Kim down into a state of alpha (I hypnotized him), and directed him through imagery and suggestions to create a good self-image of himself.

After that, I talked to him about applying for food stamps and looking into welfare. I wrote down the names of the agencies he needed to contact. I had convinced him that there was no shame in asking for help; that was what the agencies were for. He said he would contact the welfare people in the morning.

Because he was still bothered about the theft of money, I outlined a plan for him to follow. He was not to tell anyone about the theft because they wouldn't understand. Instead, he was to take four dollars a day out of his wages and slip it into the day's receipts until he had replaced all he had taken. He said he would do this, and it was apparent that he felt good about himself and the future.

Then I went home satisfied that my higher mind, expressed through me, had enriched another life.

Grandson's Eye Surgery

This case illustrates the use of group energy to achieve a desired result.

Just a couple weeks before I began writing this book, my eight-year-old grandson, Sean, had eye surgery. From this kind of surgery, the usual aftereffects for a few days are: blood seepage from the eye; swelling in and around the eye; discoloration similar to a black eye; minor, but nagging discomfort; and perhaps some temporary vision dysfunction.

The night before and morning of the surgery I went to theta and psychically sent Sean love, courage, and peace. I also mentally told him that everything would be fine and he would heal rapidly and completely.

Sean spent the night before at our house with Dee and me. Our eldest daughter Jeanne, Sean's mother, also stayed with us, so he had the benefit of being in the presence of three loving, positive auras.

Jeanne and Dee are both tuned into the powerful effects of positive energy. They and I, each in our own way, sent healing energy, love, and courage to Sean starting the night before surgery.

All three of us were with Sean prior to, during, and immediately after surgery, sending healing energy to him constantly. I went to theta when Sean returned to his room after surgery and performed psychic healing.

The results were spectacular. He had absolutely no swelling or discoloration. There was no bleeding, no discomfort, and no vision problems. There was no visible evidence of his having had surgery.

He didn't even get an upset stomach from the anesthesia. The anesthesia wore off completely in about two hours. He jumped up and said, "I want to go home." He was discharged immediately and we went home, where he began playing as though nothing had ever happened.

The more people you can get to use their psychic energy in concert, the more spectacular the results. The power of combined energies seems to increase by an order of magnitude. For instance, if one person is X-power, two persons in combined effort seem to generate X-power squared; three persons in combined effort, X to the fourth power; four persons, X to the eighth power, etc. Each additional person in a combined effort seems to cause the power factor to double over the previous power factor. It pays to work in concert with others. The possibilities of this are awesome.

If the majority of a particular race of people believe they are somehow inferior to another race, they most assuredly will perform (collectively) in such a manner as to be perceived and treated inferior by themselves and others. The few who do not subscribe to the "inferior" belief will stand out, make achievement, and be leaders. If these few leaders can use their psychic power to persuade the rest of their race that they are not inferior, stand back and watch the powerful results. As the tide of psychic energy swells in a positive direction within that race, things begin to happen not only with them, but within the world. And they will shatter the bonds of "inferiority" and assume their rightful and equal place within society. Does this ring a bell? History, including current history, is replete with the evidence of this kind of power.

As a person thinketh, so he/she is. As groups of people thinketh, so becomes the world.

Are you beginning to see now how you can use your

psychic power? Do you see how world peace can be obtained? Do you see how hunger need not be a reality in the world? Do you see how psychic power embraces everything from healing a minor paper cut to healing the world? From achieving a happy marriage to achieving a happy society? From gaining a promotion in your work to promoting harmony among all people?

In an earlier chapter, I talked about all the little bricks that composed the globe. Can you relate to that concept a little better now? You use your psychic power first to make yourself into the best possible brick; then you help others to do likewise. Thus the entire world is strengthened and made better by some measure.

By the end of this chapter, you should begin to *see*... to get a *feel* for ... to *hear* the sound of ... the message of what psychic power is all about. If you don't, I suggest you re-read the book from the beginning again before proceeding to Chapter 5, because in that chapter you are going to start learning how to develop and unleash your psychic powers. It stands to reason that you ought to have some semblance of insight before learning to use the power.

The Murder Investigation

This is the biggie! In this personal experience I used: psychometry; mental projection; telepathy; my psychic workshop; group energy projection; communication with an entity; and probably a couple other things that escape my conscious awareness at the moment.

I am deliberately vague about names, dates, gender (I refer to the victim without sexual identification), and some other physical specifics. This is so no one involved can be identified. I intend to protect them from concern and embarrassment. I have not altered any facts.

My intent is to show how you can muster a variety of psychic abilities to solve a practical problem.

I was giving a series of lectures on psychic matters. After one lecture a woman in the audience approached me. She asked if I could really get information by touching objects. This is called psychometry. I said I had had some success at it but hadn't done a lot of it. She thanked me and left.

She returned to the following night's lecture, and afterwards she again approached me.

"My husband is the homicide detective in charge of a brutal murder investigation," she said. "The police are holding the person that they are certain is the murderer on a weapons possession charge, but will have to release the person in another 48 hours if there is no physical evidence to substantiate the murder charge. My husband knows that the person will disappear immediately if released and justice may never be served."

She paused while she searched through her purse. She extracted a map which she unfolded.

"I told my husband about you," she continued. "He can use all the help he can get."

"How can I help?"

"My husband marked on the map where the body was found. Can you use psychometry and tell anything?"

"I don't know. I've never tried it before, but I will give it my best shot. No promises, though."

Standing there, I placed my right index finger on the mark on the map. I closed my eyes and went to theta. Slowly, I moved my finger around. For a minute or so, nothing happened. Then a vehicle appeared on my mental screen, and I described it to her ... color ... body style ... and even some paint scratches on one side.

"What about the bullet?" she asked. "The bullet went through the body and has not been found. The bullet is the physical evidence we need. Where is it?"

"North-northeast from the body about two hundred

yards in a clump of trees," I responded immediately because I saw it on my screen.

After that, I received nothing. She thanked me and left.

At 8 a.m. the next morning her husband phoned me. He asked if I would meet him at the murder scene. He gave me directions.

"Be sure to wear boots," he advised. "It is very muddy out there."

It was a rural area that I had never been to before. He was waiting for me with a metal detector in hand. The area was cordoned off with crime scene warnings. Little red flags were stuck in the ground where the body had been and where pieces of brain and bones had been found. It was the pattern of these pieces of brain and bone that led investigators to believe the bullet had traveled in a northwest direction. This was where they had searched in vain with metal detectors for the bullet.

The detective was warm and friendly. He looked more like a college football player than a policeman.

"Your description of the suspect's vehicle was a hundred percent accurate," he told me. "But you said the bullet traveled north-northeast. Our lab people disagree. And as you can see, there is no clump of trees in that direction."

He was right. I looked out over the barren field. There wasn't a tree in sight. Yet I had seen it clearly. And now, I felt even more strongly about it.

I began walking in the direction that I felt was correct. He slogged along with me through the mud.

About two hundred yards out, there was a sharp dip in the terrain. At the bottom of the dip was a clump of felled trees and bushes that formed a pile about three feet high and twenty feet in diameter. This had been completely hidden from view from the place where the body had lain.

"Well, I'll be . . . " he muttered.

He immediately went to work with his metal detector. I watched silently. There was no way he could penetrate the mass of brush and wood, and there was neither time nor manpower to clear it away. He only had about 24 hours left now before the suspect would have to be released.

He was frustrated. "Damn! I know it is in there, and I can't get it. I know you are right. Damn!"

"The bullet will never be found," I said. "It is too deep in the mud to be detected. Let me try a different approach."

We returned to the murder site. I went to theta and made contact with the deceased victim. The victim was confused about what had happened, but after a brief interaction I was assured that the guilty person was the one being held in jail.

"I can't go into court with that."

"I know," I laughed, "but now at least we know for sure that you are holding the right person."

"So what? We have to release the suspect in about twenty-four more hours. No physical evidence to hold him longer than that."

"Give me a moment," I said.

I went to theta again and into my psychic workshop. I called the suspect in for a visit where I did a psychic reading. When finished, I returned to beta.

"I think we have a chance at cracking this," I said. "I did a reading on the suspect and found out several very interesting things."

"Like what?"

"First, the suspect is of below-average intelligence. Second, the suspect is gloating inwardly about committing the perfect crime and making the police look like fools. Third, the suspect has an insatiable ego. The suspect loves recognition and praise."

"So?"

"So, we use that to trap him."

"How?"

"By using the combined psychic power of you, your wife, and me."

I outlined the plan. The detective and his wife both meditated regularly as a method of dealing with stress, so they already knew how to alter their consciousness.

At 8 p.m. that night they were to sit down together in their home and go into meditation. I would do the same in my home at 8 p.m. We were all to project our intelligence to the suspect's cell, and then into the suspect's mind. We were to praise the suspect lavishly about committing a brilliant, perfect crime. Then we were to lament that it was such a shame that no one would ever know about how brilliant the suspect really was. Everyone would just think of the suspect as a stupid, inept clod because they weren't aware of the suspect's cunning. Then we were to give a subtle suggestion, "If you told at least one person about your brilliant accomplishment, your brilliance would not be hidden forever."

We agreed to stay in an altered state for thirty minutes while continuously projecting the kind of thoughts I had outlined.

The news on the radio the next day told the rest of the story. The suspect had bragged about the murder in full detail to the prisoner in the adjacent cell about 9 p.m. the previous night. That morning the prisoner, who was being held for several theft charges, called the guard and offered to exchange testimony against the murder suspect in exchange for a reduction of the theft charges. The District Attorney agreed, and this was sufficient to have the murder suspect bound over for trial. Result: Conviction on first-degree murder charges and a prison sentence.

The Summary
The few brief case histories covered in this chapter and

elsewhere in this book illustrate what can be done with proper use of psychic power. As you venture into this magnificent world of the psychic, you will catalog your own encounters.

Before you turn the page and begin to learn how to become a practicing psychic, I want to prepare you for one type of experience you will encounter more often than you want to. This is the failure experience.

You will not always succeed at what you want, and you usually will not know why.

A young woman phoned me one evening for help. I had done some psychic readings for her and some of her friends quite successfully several years earlier. Now she had a serious problem. Her two-year-old daughter had been kidnapped. She and her ex-husband were involved in a bitter custody battle, and she suspected that he had taken the child. She wanted to know where the child was, if she was safe, etc. I tried daily for two weeks and drew an absolute blank every time. I was not able to help her one iota, and I felt bad about it.

I have had several people die in spite of my help. These were people who had already been declared terminally ill with no hope for survival by their physicians before I got involved. I was not tampering with their health or playing doctor. I was just trying to do what the doctors said could not be done. In those cases, the physicians were right.

When you get accustomed to dealing in the psychic realm, you begin to think that you can always rectify anything in the manner that you choose. This is not so. There is a much higher intelligence than ours, and we must defer to it. It is not our role to know everything or achieve everything in this life experience just because we want to. Our role is to do our best, offer our services with integrity, and make our mightiest effort to enrich lives and the world. Then within the framework designed by higher intelligence, we will succeed. Higher intelligence does not expect more than that from you, and you should not expect more than that from yourself.

When your efforts are unsuccessful within the framework you want, do not become discouraged. Know that the higher mind knows better, and you are working within that framework rather than the one you perceive.

Then forget the matter, and go on to continue offering your best efforts wherever you find the opportunity.

Now turn the page and learn how to develop your own psychic ability.

CHAPTER 5

BECOMING A PSYCHIC

Preparation and Ground Rules

This is the chapter you have been waiting for—exact instructions on how to awaken your innate psychic abilities and become a practicing psychic. Once you develop this skill, there is virtually no limit as to what you can experience and do.

Do not begin to perform the instructions in this chapter until you have read the entire book and have given serious thought to everything discussed. This is a serious commitment, and it will not work unless you enter into it with integrity, dedication, and a sincere desire to enrich yourself and all with whom you interact.

The series of 30 psychic development sessions given in this chapter is carefully structured to awaken and sharpen your innate psychic abilities so you can become a practicing psychic in your everyday life. Since no two people are alike, there are no guarantees as to precisely what each individual will achieve from these sessions. However, there are a few simple rules that *must* be followed in order to achieve the best results for you. If you do not follow the rules, your results may be less than your maximum potential; you may not even have any significant results at all. Please, for the sake of your development, follow the rules.

Rule #1: You must complete each session in sequence without skipping a session. That is, session #1 first, then #2, then #3, and so forth through session #30. Also, you must not switch sessions around.

Rule #2: You must wait at least one hour between sessions.

Rule #3: You must not allow more than one calendar day to lapse between sessions.

Rule #4: If you do allow more than one day to lapse between sessions, you must begin your program completely over starting with session #1. There are no exceptions to this rule.

Rule #5: If you do skip a session (for example you skip from session 5 to session 7 without doing 6 in between), you must begin your program completely over starting with session #1. There are no exceptions to this rule.

Rule #6: Immediately after each session you must write on a paper a little handwriting exercise that will be explained very shortly.

Rule #7: If you skip a handwriting exercise, you must begin your program over starting with session #1. There are no exceptions to this rule. The handwriting exercise is a vital part of the training and must be taken seriously.

(*Note:* These seven rules apply only the *first* time you go through the training program. Once you have completed all 30 sessions, following all the rules exactly, then you can go back and refresh or reinforce yourself with any of the sessions in any order you wish, any time you wish.)

The longest it can take you to complete the psychic training is 30 days if you do only one session a day for 30 consecutive days. If it takes longer, it means you are skipping sessions and having to restart.

The shortest it can take you to complete the psychic training is less than two days. I don't recommend this because you wouldn't have time to eat or sleep properly to meet that sort of schedule. A more practical schedule might be two or three sessions a day, which would allow you to complete the training in 10 to 15 days.

You need a cassette tape recorder and some inexpensive blank tapes. You will also need a sheet of writing paper and either a pen or a pencil. You will want a relatively quiet place to do these exercises and to ask others not to disturb you during the exercise. Take the phone off the hook. Most exercises can be done in about 20 to 30 minutes. This is a small amount of time to invest for such a great potential payback.

Each exercise is to be done as follows:

1. The words in italics for each day are the ones you are to record on a tape. Speak slowly, in your normal speaking voice, at a pace that is comfortable for you. Pause or stop speaking, while allowing the tape to continue running, in the places I indicate in the instructions.

2. Sit in a comfortable chair. I recommend a straight-backed, armless chair. Rewind the tape you just recorded and set it within arm's reach so you can play the tape back to yourself.

3. Place the sheet of paper and a pen or a pencil within arm's reach. You will need them after you listen to the tape.

4. Turn the recorder to PLAY, close your eyes and relax. Listen to the tape and follow the directions on the tape.

5. When finished with the tape, open your eyes and immediately write the following on the sheet of paper: *Session 1* (or whatever the appropriate session is) *is completed.* Then write the date and sign your name in your normal writing script, with the following modifications:

   a. All i-dots are to be tiny circles placed slightly above the i-stem, neither ahead of nor in back of the i-stem. Like this:

   b. All t-bar crossings are to be placed at the top of the t-stem and should be long, firm left-to-right strokes. Like this:

   c. Your signature is to be underscored with a firm left-to-right stroke. Like this:

   William W. Hewitt

   d. You should write with a firm pressure, not lightly. If you can feel the indention on the backside of the paper, that is very good.

   The complete message you write after each session should look something like this:

   Session #6 is completed.
   July 4, 1987
   William W. Hewitt

Of course, do not copy my handwriting except for the modifications mentioned above. Use your own handwriting and your own signature.

This writing exercise is extremely important and must not be omitted. The exercise, with the modifications I gave, will strengthen your self-confidence, enthusiasm, tenacity, imagination, and creativity. These are all traits that are a must in order to be a good psychic. As a bonus, the writing exercise also provides a log of your progress so you don't inadvertently lose track or skip a session.

In the beginning, you may find it difficult to alter your writing to incorporate the modifications. Just keep at it faithfully. By the end of 30 consecutive sessions, it will be a natural part of your script. I recommend that you are to continue writing with these modifications permanently after the 30-session program.

The Psychic World

As a psychic practitioner, you will sometimes encounter experiences that are quite startling. Once you have gained some experience, you will easily handle whatever occurs without any undue concern. But in the beginning phases of your learning, some experiences can be quite upsetting. I want to alert you to this before you start the 30-session program because you may well encounter some unusual experiences during the training, and I don't want you to let it frighten you and prevent you from continuing to pursue the training. Here is one such experience I had.

In February 1972 I was just starting as a practicing psychic. A man came to me and asked me to tune in to his eight-year-old niece who lived in another state. I was not emotionally prepared for what happened.

I altered my consciousness to the theta level and invoked the image of the little girl. She appeared, and within seconds I watched her wither up and die. Then I saw a casket with a calendar on top of it. The calendar said May 2, 1972. I began to weep profusely over the death of this beautiful child. I was emotionally shaken to the bones. (*Note*: the theta level is where all our emotions are recorded.)

I remained in theta and explored the child; I discovered that she had leukemia. I then attempted to perform psychic healing for her benefit. I say "attempted" because I was stopped almost immediately by a command from my higher self to not interfere in this case because the death was necessary for reasons that did not concern me. This caused me to weep uncontrollably. My face was wet, and I could feel the tears dripping onto my chest and lap.

Remaining in theta, I then directed love, courage, and peace to the child. When I felt that she had indeed received and accepted the love, courage, and peace I brought myself out of theta and into beta. Then I opened my eyes. I was still crying. It was a minute or so before I gained control of my emotions and could speak.

Her uncle's face was ashen. He knew from my visible reaction that something was wrong. I told him everything. He then told me he had feared something was wrong, and that was why he had come to me. It seems he had visited his brother and sister-in-law and their child the previous week. The child had become sickly, but the parents refused to take her to a doctor. He said his brother and sister-in-law were miserly cheap even though they were financially sound. They weren't going to "throw good money to a doctor when all that was wrong was a little head cold."

I advised him to get the child to a doctor immediately. He said he was going to fly back to Texas in the morning and personally take the child to a doctor and pay the bill himself.

Several weeks later, the uncle contacted me and confirmed that he had done just as he had vowed. The parents let him take the child for medical attention as long as he agreed to pay all expenses. The prognosis was grim. The child had terminal leukemia.

In May, the uncle again contacted me to let me know the child had died on May 2.

There are several things to learn from this case history.

1. You may very well encounter experiences that will shake you up. Through experience and sufficient precondi-

tioning of yourself, you will learn to handle anything. So do not let these experiences deter you from practicing and progressing.

2. You are not always able to help in the manner you would like to. I was thwarted in my efforts to perform psychic healing by a higher power that had a more complete understanding of the case than I did.

3. You can always send love, courage, and peace to anyone, any place, any time without restriction. And this includes drawing in generous portions of love, courage, and peace to yourself from the infinite source. I heartily recommend you develop the daily habit of sending these energies to others and to yourself.

4. Sometimes you experience things exactly as they are, and sometimes you experience symbols or an event that is a shorthand version of a situation. In this instance, I had all three elements. The quick withering away was a shorthand version of what would happen over the next several months. The casket symbolized death. The calendar reflected exactly the time of death.

You have to be careful in interpreting symbols. In this case, I correctly interpreted the casket as meaning physical death. Several years later, while doing a projection forward in time, I encountered a person and a casket. Again, I interpreted this as the physical death of that person. I was wrong. What actually occurred was the death of that person's profound negativism and self-destructive thought patterns. Had I been more careful and thorough in my psychic investigation of that person I would have discovered the truth. Instead I had jumped to a conclusion because a casket had once been correctly indicative of physical death. I learned a valuable lesson. Fortunately, I had not told anyone about the "death," so no harm was done. So learn from my mistake—be cautious, thorough, and very discreet about pronouncing a verdict of death. I have since adopted a rule to never mention physical death when I see it unless there are some exceptionally compelling reasons to do so. So far, I have not encountered sufficiently compelling reasons.

Another kind of unexpected encounter that I want to caution you about is one that can be terrifying.

Sometimes when you enter the psychic world you inadvertently enter one of the lower astral planes that is inhabited by extremely negative energies.

For most people, no harm can come of these encounters other than having the daylights scared out of you. There is a way to handle these encounters that will be programmed in during one of the training sessions.

Quite simply, you just point your finger and then snap your fingers at the energy that is threatening to you. Each time you point and snap, the energy decreases in size fifty percent. So you rapidly point and snap, point and snap, etc., until the energy just disappears. As an aside, this is excellent for teaching children to rid them of their nightmares.

I said "most" people cannot be harmed in these encounters. That means some can be. There are only four ways that there is potential danger, the danger being that one of these energies enters and possesses your body.

1. You are out of control due to alcohol or drugs.

2. Through ignorance, you actually invite the energy to enter.

3. Through fear, you are intimidated into inviting the energy to enter.

4. You have a defect in your aura due to some grave personality defect such as schizophrenia.

Item #1 is easily handled. Just do not enter the psychic world if you are using drugs or alcohol. If you do enter while under the influence, that does not mean you will become possessed. It means that the risk is there, and it could happen. It is not worth the risk.

Item #2 is being handled by your reading this book and becoming informed. You know that the energy cannot enter you unless you actually invite it in. So don't invite it. It's that simple.

Item #3 is also handled by this book if you complete the 30-session training program. You will be programmed to handle fear. And, again, don't invite the energy in. You are in control, and no one or no thing has the right to intimidate you unless you willingly allow it.

Item #4 is something that I am not able to help you with. People in this category are in much more danger of possession than all other groups combined. And I don't know how to prevent it except to say that if you have some grave personality disorder, do not practice psychic excursions. This advice is sort of like whistling into the wind because people with that sort of problem are not going to take my advice anyway.

Let's continue discussing negative energy but from a different perspective.

Every person in the world is an energy source. That means both positive and negative energy. The negative energies from other people cannot harm you unless you allow it. We will program in a shield of protection against the negative energies during the 30-session program.

Of greater concern is the negative energy *you* generate. If you generate negative energy, it will, just like the proverbial chickens, come home to roost. You cannot protect yourself from your own negative energy. You created it ... you own it ... and you must deal with it sooner or later in some fashion.

Before you panic, let me say that there are effective ways to counteract the negative energy that you generate so that you do not have to bear the full brunt of its return.

In essence, what you do is to override the negative with massive positive energy.

A simplistic example: you speak unjustly about a person and cause him problems (you created a negative energy, or karma) and thus create the need for a counterbalancing positive energy (karma). If you do nothing, the negative karma will return to you in some manner . . . perhaps you will be unjustly lied about . . . perhaps something else. The Law of Ten-Fold applies to negative karma as well as to positive karma so you could well receive ten times the return. However, this does not have to be. You can avert the negative karma by creating overriding positive karma. In this example, you might do something like the following.

Alter your state of consciousness and:

1. Forgive yourself and ask forgiveness of the person you wronged through the higher mind which embraces both of you.
2. Send love, courage, and peace to the person you wronged.
3. Correct the situation completely for the wronged person by visualizing him as having his reputation restored and having increased respect given him by others, etc.
4. Program yourself to become immediately aware when you are about to create negative energy so that you can immediately stop it through that awareness. Ask your higher mind to empower you to control yourself better.

You will want to repeat steps 1, 2, and 3 over a several-day period, depending on the severity of the situation you caused. Once is sufficient for minor infractions.

Of course, if there is something physical that needs balancing you should do that also. For example, you stole a neighbor's tool box. Either return it, or send an appropriate amount of money anonymously in the mail. This is in addition to the psychic steps lis

By using your positive
sometimes eliminate the ne
tive counterbalancing as a
tive action.

ONE CAUTION: Dc
as a way of doing whatev
escaping the consequen
quences. Your psychic ab
continued misuse of it brings a karm
but must be experienced. Psychic ability must be u
a sense of responsibility and integrity. If not, you will have
to learn your lesson through a very difficult route. Do not
let that happen to you. Remember, you always have a
choice. Choose wisely.

Session #1

Purpose: This first programming session is to condition your body and mind for deep relaxation. Deep relaxation automatically triggers your mind to enter the alpha and
theta ranges. Even if you already meditate or use other
relaxation methods, you must perform this first session.
That is because of the building block structure mentioned
earlier.

Most likely you will enter some level of alpha rather
than theta during this exercise. Eventually, in a subsequent
session, you will have your mind conditioned sufficiently
to enter theta easily.

Preparation: Get your tape recorder, a blank tape,
paper and pen or pencil, a comfortable chair, and as quiet a
location as you can. Take the phone off the hook.

Record the session written in italics in the **Programming Cycle** section by reading the words out loud and

...n on a cassette tape. Where instructions say ...p talking for about three seconds or so while the ...nues to run. Then resume reading the italicized ...For longer pauses, the instructions will say STOP ...ING FOR X SECONDS while letting the tape con-...ue to run. You can either use a watch or just count slowly (silently) to approximate the number of seconds. In place of X, the instructions will specify a number such as 10.

Programming Cycle: After you have recorded the following instructions (only record the italicized words), rewind the tape. Then relax in your chair, turn your recorder to PLAY, close your eyes and listen to the tape and follow the instructions given on the tape.

Take a deep breath and allow yourself to begin to relax. PAUSE *I want you to imagine now. In your mind's eye, visualize yourself sitting comfortably in your chair as you are at this moment. Imagine a valve on the top of your head. Attached to the valve is a balloon. The balloon is not inflated at this moment. This is an unbreakable balloon. In a few moments you will allow all of your tension, fears, worries, troubles, and negativism to leave your body and enter the balloon.* PAUSE
Imagine now that a soft, gentle steady pressure is starting in the soles of your feet. PAUSE *Feel this pressure pushing upward in your feet, pushing all tension, fear, worry, trouble, and negativism ahead of it. Pushing up into your ankles and calves. As the pressure pushes steadily upward, the balloon begins to inflate as tension, fear, worry, troubles, and negativism flow from the top of your head into the balloon. See the balloon inflating slowly.* PAUSE
The area behind the moving pressure becomes relaxed and numb because the tension is gone. Your feet and ankles and calves are relaxed and numb. PAUSE *Feel the soft, gentle pressure move up into your thighs.* PAUSE *Relaxing your thighs.* PAUSE *See the balloon inflate even more.* PAUSE *Allow the pressure to con-*

tinue to flow in its upward movement. *Relaxing your hips. Relaxing your waist. See the balloon getting larger with the grayish-black unwanted negativism, fear, tension, worries, and troubles that you once had.* PAUSE

The pressure moves up through your chest area, relaxing your lungs, relaxing your heart, relaxing all the organs within the trunk of your body. Your body is clear and numb and relaxed. The balloon is getting quite large as all the dirty, unwanted crud is forced out the top of your head and into the balloon. The pressure moves through your shoulders and into your neck, relaxing your neck. Your neck becomes rubbery with relaxation and your head droops slightly. PAUSE

Another soft, gentle pressure begins in your fingertips and moves upward through your hands, wrists, arms, shoulders and into your neck to blend in with the other relaxing pressure there. You are completely relaxed and clear and numb from toes to neck now. The balloon is very large now with its undesirable cargo of negativism, fear, tension, worry, and troubles. Now your gentle pressure makes its final surge upward completely through your head, forcing every trace of fear, negativism, worry, tension, and trouble from your body and into the balloon. Now reach up and shut off the valve on top of your head so none of the balloon's contents can leak back. PAUSE *Now take a strong nylon rope and tie the neck of the balloon tightly closed.* PAUSE

Now reach up and push the balloon free from the valve so it can float up and away from you, carrying with it all the undesirable cargo that you have evacuated from your entire being. PAUSE *Watch the balloon float further and further up and away until it is completely out of sight, never to return. You are happy to be rid of the cargo the balloon carried away.* PAUSE *Your entire being is now clean, clear, and free. You are relaxed from toes to head. Your mind has altered your consciousness to a healthy level in the alpha range.* PAUSE

Imagine now that the Sun is poised just above your head. In the center of the Sun is the number 3. See it. PAUSE *Feel the*

warmth as it relaxes the top of your head. PAUSE *Now allow the Sun with the number 3 to enter your head and move slowly down through your body, bringing with it even greater relaxation and an even deeper level of mind. Down through your face and neck. Down through your shoulders, arms, and hands. The Sun and number 3 move down through your chest, relaxing all the organs within your chest even more. Down through your waist, hips, thighs, knees, calves, ankles, feet, and toes. Relaxing you completely. Now mentally repeat the number 3 while visualizing it.* PAUSE *In the future, all you need to do to reach this level of mind or an even deeper level is to mentally visualize and repeat the number 3.* PAUSE

Now visualize the Sun once again poised above your head. This time the Sun has the number 2 imprinted on it. See it. PAUSE *Feel the relaxing warmth.* PAUSE *Allow this number 2 Sun to move down into your head and progress downward through your body, bringing with it an even deeper level of mind and even greater relaxation than the number 3 Sun. Down through your face, neck, shoulders, chest. Notice the golden glow that seems to fill your entire being as this number 2 Sun moves through you. Down through your waist, hips, thighs, knees, calves, ankles, feet and toes. You are now in a great state of relaxation, and your mind is at an even deeper level of consciousness. Deeper than before. Now mentally repeat the number 2 while visualizing it.* PAUSE *In the future, when you mentally visualize and repeat the number 2 you will enter a level of mind that is as deep as you are now or even deeper.* PAUSE

One more time visualize the Sun poised above your head. This time the Sun has the number 1 emblazoned on it. PAUSE *See it. Feel it.* PAUSE *This is the most powerful of all the Suns. It is brighter, more relaxing, and more mind deepening than any. Allow this number 1 Sun to enter your head and move downward through your body, bringing with it total relaxation, profound deepening of your consciousness, and total purity. I will stop talking now for a short time while you guide your number 1 Sun com-*

pletely through your body to your toes. STOP TALKING FOR 20 SECONDS WHILE ALLOWING THE TAPE TO CONTINUE RUNNING. THIS ALLOWS TIME FOR YOU TO PERFORM THE INSTRUCTIONS.

You are now at the deepest level of consciousness and relaxation that you have ever experienced. Mentally visualize and repeat the number 1. Any time in the future that you mentally visualize and repeat the number 1, you will go as deep as you are now or even deeper.

In the future, all you need to do to reach this level or a deeper level is to close your eyes, take a deep breath, allow yourself to relax, and mentally visualize and repeat the number 3, then visualize and repeat the number 2, then visualize and repeat the number 1. PAUSE *Take a deep breath now, and go deeper.* PAUSE *I am now going to count from 1 to 5. At the count of 5 you will open your eyes and be wide awake and feeling fine. One.* PAUSE *Two.* PAUSE *Three. You are coming up slowly.* PAUSE *Four.* PAUSE *Five. Open eyes. Wide awake and feeling fine.*

After Programming: Take your pen/pencil and paper and write the following—Session #1 is completed. Write the date. Sign your name. Be sure to use the writing modifications described earlier in this chapter. Then keep your paper as your record of achievement so you do not inadvertently skip a session.

Optional Additional Programming: If you wish, you can record the following instructions and execute them just as you did for the main programming cycle. Do not substitute this exercise for the main programming cycle listed above. This is just an additional exercise in case you want to hone yourself even more. You don't have to perform this optional exercise, but I recommend that you do if you have the extra time available to you. You can gain much if you do perform it, but you will not lose anything if you don't. Be sure you have performed the main programming cycle (above) before you do this optional one. This exercise is good for training your mind to visualize and to respond to your command. It also deepens your level of consciousness.

Close your eyes and take a deep breath. PAUSE *Mentally visualize and repeat the number 3.* PAUSE *Mentally visualize and repeat the number 2.* PAUSE *Mentally visualize and repeat the number 1.* PAUSE *You are now at a deep, healthy level of mind. Take a deep breath and go deeper.* PAUSE *Now visualize a black chalkboard similar to the kind you had in school.* PAUSE *The chalkboard has a chalk tray. In the chalk tray are an eraser and several pieces of white chalk.* PAUSE

Pick up a piece of chalk and draw a large circle on the board. PAUSE *Now print the number 10 inside the circle.* PAUSE *Now erase the number 10 from inside the circle but do not erase the circle.* PAUSE *Print the number 9 inside the circle.* PAUSE *Erase the 9.* PAUSE *Print 8 inside the circle.* PAUSE *Erase the 8.* PAUSE *Print 7.* PAUSE *Erase the 7.* PAUSE *Print 6.* PAUSE *Erase the 6.* PAUSE *Print 5.* PAUSE *Erase the 5.* PAUSE *Print 4.* PAUSE *Erase the 4.* PAUSE *Print 3.* PAUSE *Erase the 3.* PAUSE *Print 2.* PAUSE *Erase the 2.* PAUSE *Print 1.* PAUSE *Erase the 1.* PAUSE

Now erase the circle and erase the picture of the chalkboard from your mind. PAUSE *Now count yourself up from 1 to 5 and open your eyes.*

Comments: This programming session starts training your mind to alter your state of consciousness at your command. It also starts training your visualization faculties, which are important for good psychic performance. The procedure also programs in a shorter method (3-2-1 countdown) of relaxing and altering your state of consciousness.

The main procedure and the optional procedure are

both excellent for general relaxation and releasing tension. If you feel the need, you can use these as often as you wish, any time you wish.

Session #2

Purpose: In this session you will enter the skyscraper of your consciousness. You will enter deepest alpha, and will program in a short method of returning quickly to deepest alpha whenever you wish. Your skyscraper of consciousness is a place you will go to from now on. This is the next building block step toward entering theta, which you will accomplish in Session #3.

Preparation: Get your tape recorder, a blank tape, paper and pen or pencil, a comfortable chair, and as quiet a location as you can. Take the phone off the hook.

Record the session written in italics in the **Programming Cycle** section by reading the words out loud and recording them on a cassette tape. Where instructions say PAUSE, stop talking for about three seconds or so while the tape continues to run. Then resume reading the italicized words. For longer pauses, the instructions will say STOP TALKING FOR X SECONDS while letting the tape continue to run. You can either use a watch or just count slowly (silently) to approximate the number of seconds. In place of X, the instructions will specify a number such as 10.

Programming Cycle: After you have recorded the following instructions (only record the italicized words), rewind the tape. Then relax in your chair, turn your recorder to PLAY, close your eyes and listen to the tape and follow the instructions given on the tape.

Take a deep breath and mentally visualize and repeat the number 3 as you exhale. PAUSE *Take another deep breath and* mentally visualize and repeat the number 2 as you exhale. PAUSE Take one more deep breath and mentally visualize and repeat the number 1 as you exhale. PAUSE

You have now entered an altered state of consciousness by the 3-2-1 method. In the future you will merely be instructed to enter your altered state by the 3-2-1 method, and you will be expected to perform the 3-2-1 countdown and visualization by yourself. You will always enter a level that is as deep as, or deeper than, you are at now. A very relaxing, healthy, beneficial state. Each breath you take relaxes you even more and takes you deeper.

Imagine now that you are standing in front of an infinitely tall skyscraper. PAUSE Look up. It is so tall that the top disappears into the clouds and beyond. PAUSE Now look back down to the street level entrance into the skyscraper. Your name is boldly printed above the entrance. PAUSE See your name above the entrance. PAUSE This is your building. It is the skyscraper of your mind . . . of your consciousness. PAUSE Now walk inside your skyscraper into the ground floor. PAUSE You are inside now. Look around you. You have been here before. PAUSE

This is where you have spent much of your life in the past, living day to day, battling problems the hard way, winning some, losing some. Beginning now, you intend to start using more and more of your mind. This means opening more doors in your skyscraper of consciousness. This means going to any higher level of your consciousness that you wish whenever you wish. Your goal is to enrich your life and the lives of others by more extensive and efficient use of your mind and its innate psychic power. PAUSE

At the other end of the room are two elevator doors. One is labeled UP ONLY and the other DOWN ONLY. See them. PAUSE Walk over to the one labeled DOWN ONLY. PAUSE There is an unbreakable padlock on a small table near the door. PAUSE Pick up the padlock and put it on the DOWN ONLY elevator door and snap it shut into the locked position. PAUSE You know where the DOWN elevator goes because you have been there before. It is not a nice place down there, and you have no intention of ever going *there again. You are glad the door is locked and that you do not have a key for the lock.*

Now walk to the UP ONLY door. It automatically opens for you. Walk into the elevator and push the UP button. The elevator door closes and you start moving to a higher level of consciousness. PAUSE The elevator stops at a door labeled DEEPEST ALPHA. Your name is printed on the door also. Read your name. PAUSE Now the door slides open revealing a short hallway. On the floor just outside the elevator is a painted white square with a red number 10 in the center. Step out of the elevator onto the square. PAUSE

You are now on the number 10 square. The elevator door closes behind you. Look ahead down the hallway. There seem to be more squares with numbers on them. The next numbered square from you is white with an orange number 9 on it. It is just one step from you. Remaining on the number 10 square, take a deep breath and say 10 and mentally visualize a red 10 while exhaling. PAUSE Feel yourself going deeper. PAUSE Now step onto the orange 9 square. Take a deep breath and say 9 and mentally visualize an orange 9 while exhaling. PAUSE Feel yourself going deeper still. Your mind is adjusting in the direction of deepest alpha toward your ultimate level of psychic awareness.

One step further is a square with a yellow number 8. Step onto the 8 and mentally say 8 while visualizing a yellow 8. PAUSE You continue to go deeper. Everything around you is warm and hazy. All you can see is the next number, which is a green 7. Step onto the 7 and go deeper while saying and visualizing a green 7. PAUSE Next is a blue 6. Step to 6 while saying 6 and visualizing a blue 6. PAUSE Go deeper. Now go to the indigo 5 while saying 5 and visualizing the deep indigo blue 5. PAUSE Deeper and deeper. Now go to the violet 4 while saying 4 and visualizing the violet 4. PAUSE

Go deeper. Now your vision in front of you clears. Immediately in front of you are three golden steps down. In front of the bottom step is a door labeled TO THETA with your name also printed *on it. A silver nail is on the wall next to the door, and a golden key hangs on the nail. PAUSE You are just three short steps away from deepest alpha and the threshold entrance to theta. Take a step down now. Down to 3 and mentally visualize and repeat the number 3. PAUSE Now down to 2 and mentally visualize and repeat the number 2. PAUSE Step down to 1 and mentally visualize and repeat the number 1. PAUSE*

You are now in deepest alpha at the threshold of theta, which is your best psychic level. In the future, whenever you count down from 3 to 1 while visualizing and repeating the numbers 3-2-1, you will enter deepest alpha at the threshold of theta just as you are now. The door in front of you leads to theta and into the world of psychic experience. The golden key unlocks the door. In the next session, Session #3, you will return here to open the door and enter the psychic realm. PAUSE

Now it is time to return to the beta level of consciousness in the ground floor of your skyscraper of consciousness. Use the 1 to 5 countout method. Say one, feel yourself drifting back down the hallway toward your elevator. Say two as your elevator returns toward beta. Say three and your elevator door opens at your beta level. Say four as you step from the elevator. Say five and open your eyes. Wide awake and feeling fine.

After Programming: Take your pen/pencil and paper and write the following—Session #2 is completed. Write the date. Sign your name. Be sure to use the writing modifications described earlier in this chapter. Then keep your paper as your record of achievement so you do not inadvertently skip a session.

Optional Additional Programming: This is an optional extra to help you tune yourself up even more. Do not substitute this exercise for the main programming cycle listed above. This is just an additional exercise if you want to hone yourself even more. You don't have to perform this optional

exercise, but I recomn
time available to you. Yo
it, but you will not lose a
　Take yourself to the c
countdown method you lea
ming cycle. Then visualize t.
attention focused on thoughts c
to visualize and think whatever lc
as long as you wish in this altered st.
and visualizing LOVE. If your thou　　　　　　　　ɔn
start to drift away from LOVE, you sho　　　　　　ɪ mind
back by once again visualizing the worc　　　ɪ. Do this as
often as necessary to train your mind to fcʊs on what you
want. This exercise helps discipline your mind while enrich-
ing yourself with the most powerful, positive energy of
all . . . LOVE. Count yourself out with the 1 to 5 method
when you are ready to return to beta. If you remain in alpha
for an extended period of time you may find yourself drifting back toward beta before you want to. That is OK. Let it
happen. Just experience it. You can always return to deepest
alpha later. Eventually, as you become more experienced,
you will learn to drop the 1 to 5 countout and just go to beta
in an instant by an act of will.

　Comments: In this session you took a significant step
toward reaching your level of psychic functioning. This session disciplined your mind more, took you much deeper
into alpha (a higher level of conscious awareness), and
honed your visualization even more. If your visualization is
not as clear or vivid as you want, do not be concerned. Just
perform the exercises with your best effort. Your visualization will improve; part of the purpose of these exercises is
to train your mind to visualize at your command.
　In the next session you will enter theta and into your
psychic workshop. From that point on, all exercises will

take place in your

psychic workshop.

Session #3

Purpose: In this session you will enter your theta region, create your personal psychic workshop, and program in some protective safeguards for yourself and others. After this session you will always go to your psychic workshop for all your psychic work.

Preparation: Get your tape recorder, a blank tape, paper and pen or pencil, a comfortable chair, and as quiet a location as you can. Take the phone off the hook.

Record the session written in italics under **Programming Cycle** by reading the words out loud and recording them on a cassette tape. Where instructions say PAUSE, stop talking for about three seconds or so while the tape continues to run. Then resume reading the italicized words. For longer pauses, the instructions will say STOP TALKING FOR X SECONDS while letting the tape continue to run. You can either use a watch or just count slowly (silently) to approximate the number of seconds. In place of X, the instructions will specify a number such as 10.

Programming Cycle: After you have recorded the following instructions (only record the italicized words), rewind the tape. Then relax in your chair, turn on your recorder to PLAY, close your eyes and listen to the tape and follow the instructions given on the tape.

Enter your deepest alpha level in your infinite skyscraper of consciousness by the 3-2-1 method. I will stop talking for a short time while you do this. STOP TALKING FOR 45 SECONDS WHILE ALLOWING THE TAPE TO CONTINUE RUNNING. *You are now at your deepest alpha level in your infinite skyscraper of consciousness. There is a door in front of you labeled TO THETA and your name is on the door.* PAUSE *Hanging on a silver nail next to the door is a key.* PAUSE *See the door and the gold key.* PAUSE *Now reach up and take the key from the nail and unlock the door.* PAUSE *Push the door open fully.* PAUSE *Take one step through the door and stand there.* PAUSE *You are standing at the top of a spiral staircase that is constructed of clear material which radiates soft, psychic, ultra-violet light. The staircase has ten steps winding gently to the bottom. At this moment you are unable to see beyond the bottom of the staircase because the relaxing ultra-violet light creates a beautiful velvety fog that hides the view beyond. Stand here a moment and look at the radiating staircase and the soft violet fog.* STOP TALKING FOR 5 SECONDS WHILE THE TAPE CONTINUES TO RUN.

Take a step down to the ninth step now. PAUSE *Feel the psychic violet light caress you and take you down quickly to a deeper level of mind.* PAUSE *Now step down to the eighth step. Deeper into the psychic fog and into a deeper level of consciousness.* PAUSE *Step down to seven. Deeper still. Down to six.* PAUSE *Five.* PAUSE *Four.* PAUSE *Three.* PAUSE *Two.* PAUSE *One.*

You are now at the bottom of your psychic staircase and are in the theta region of your consciousness. The violet fog lifts, revealing that you are standing in front of a door labeled PSYCHIC WORK-SHOP. Your name is also on the door. PAUSE *Open the door, and from the room beyond the door a flood of pure white light comes streaming out through the open doorway. Walk into the room, into the pure white light.* PAUSE *You are in the room now. Look around you. This is your psychic workshop. Your own personal place in your consciousness where you can come whenever you wish.*

You are free here. Free to create. Free to be who you are. Free to do whatever you want. The pure white light in this room seems to be everywhere, yet there seems to be no light source. This is your pure psychic light which comprises all frequencies and fills you with ability to perform as a psychic for any worthwhile purpose. Stand a moment and allow the light to go in through every pore in your skin, filling you completely. PAUSE *You are filled with the light. You are clear and radiant. You are filled with psychic power.* PAUSE

Now walk into the center of the room. Create a chair for yourself there. Make it comfortable. Make it the material, color and design of your choice. STOP TALKING FOR 10 SECONDS WHILE THE TAPE CONTINUES TO RUN. *Now sit down in your chair.* PAUSE *If you are right-handed, create one all-purpose control button at the right hand side of your chair. If you are left-handed create the all-purpose control button at the left.* STOP TALKING FOR 6 SECONDS. TAPE STILL RUNNING. *This button enables you to bring anything you command into or out of your psychic workshop. To test your button, mentally say "I want a chalkboard," and press the button. Allow the chalkboard to descend from the ceiling and appear in front of you where you can use it.* PAUSE

Now say, "Go back," and press the button and watch the chalkboard raise up and out of sight. PAUSE *You can raise and lower a movie screen the same way. You can open and close that door straight ahead of you at the far end of your workshop. You are in absolute control here. I am going to stop talking for a minute while you explore your psychic workshop and create anything in it you desire.* STOP TALKING FOR 60 SECONDS WHILE THE TAPE CONTINUES TO RUN.

Now it is time to do some psychic work. If you have not finished furnishing your workshop, do not be concerned. You will be back here many times in the future and will have ample opportunity to do whatever you wish. Now find a comfortable position in your chair. PAUSE *Mentally say, "I want my protective psychic shield," and then press your button. A shield of power descends from the ceiling and drops over your head and envelopes your entire body.* PAUSE *The energy is transparent. You can see it vibrating, yet you can easily see through it. You can feel the positive attraction.* PAUSE

Now the energy shrinks in closer and closer until it blends into your body and you can no longer see it. It is part of you now forever. This psychic shield will not allow external negative energy to penetrate and do you harm. You will be able to see external negative

influences. You will be able to feel or sense the presence of external negative energy, and you will be able to successfully deal with external negative energy. But the detrimental effects of any external negative energy cannot penetrate your shield and cause you harm, and this is so. PAUSE

If you generate harmful negative energy, it cannot pass through your shield and harm others. This means you will temporarily lose your psychic power if you try to use it in a harmful way. You must take great care to not generate negative energy because it will remain trapped within your own shield where you must deal with it. You can deal with your own negative energy by overriding it with positive energy and action. You have already studied this and are aware of what to do.

You now have shielded yourself from harmful external energies, and you have shielded yourself so you cannot cause harm to others. Only one other protective device is needed. In the rare case that you should encounter some sort of demonic energy from a lower astral plane, you need a method of quickly getting rid of it. If you ever encounter a demonic energy, point your finger boldly at it, snap your fingers, and mentally command "Shrink!" The demon will shrink to half its size and power. Point and snap again and command "Shrink!" once more. The demon will shrink fifty percent again.

Keep repeatedly pointing, snapping, and shouting "Shrink!" until it either disappears completely or becomes so small and powerless that you have no need for concern. Always remember, you are in control. Even if you do not use the finger point-snap-shout technique, the demon cannot harm you because of your shield. It can only make you feel uncomfortable. PAUSE

There is one important thing you need to know before you leave your psychic workshop for now and return to beta level. Your workshop has the ability to automatically transport you to the proper level of consciousness in your psychic skyscraper for whatever you are doing. You need not be concerned about levels any longer. While in your workshop, you will be instantly adjusted to wherever you need to be. PAUSE

Now take one last look around. PAUSE *You like being here.* PAUSE *Now walk to your spiral psychic staircase. Slowly go up the stairs, counting from 1 to 10 as you step up each step.* STOP TALKING FOR 10 SECONDS WHILE THE TAPE CONTINUES TO RUN. *You are at the top of your staircase now.* PAUSE *Now use your 1 to 5 countout to return to the ground floor of your psychic sky-scraper and into the beta level.*

After Programming: Take your pen/pencil and paper and write the following—Session #3 is completed. Write the date. Sign your name. Be sure to use the writing modifications described earlier in this chapter. Then keep your paper as your record of achievement so you do not inadvertently skip a session.

Optional Additional Programming: This is an optional extra to help you tune yourself up even more. Do not substitute this exercise for the main programming cycle listed above. This is just an additional exercise if you want to hone yourself even more. You don't have to perform this optional exercise, but I recommend that you do if you have the extra time available to you. You can gain much if you do perform it, but you will not lose anything if you don't.

Take yourself to deepest alpha by the 3-2-1 countdown method. Then enter your psychic workshop by counting down from 10 to 1 as you descend the ten steps of your psychic spiral staircase just as you learned in the main programming cycle (above). Stay in your workshop and explore it. Finish bringing things in that you want. For example, you may want a cabinet that has every psychic wonder medication you could ever want. You may want additional chairs or a sofa. Perhaps some special paintings. Perhaps a library that contains all information you could ever want. Perhaps a computer. Or maybe you don't want much at all in there. It is your choice.

Before you leave, just relax in your chair and allow your mind to drift to any pleasant thought while you soak up the powerful energy in this room. When you are ready to leave, climb your staircase counting 1 to 10 as you do. At the top of the staircase, bring yourself back to beta by the 1 to 5 countout.

Comments: You can enter your workshop as often as you wish any time. This is where you will go for all psychic performance. You have probably noticed how much faster you enter deep levels of alpha and theta. At some future time, you will be able to do it instantly with your eyes open or closed. More on this at the end of this chapter. For a while you must be content with a countdown procedure as you are being taught.

Session #4

Purpose: In this session you will learn one method of programming goals. You will also establish a personal creed and motto to guide you in your future psychic work.

Preparation: Get your tape recorder, a blank tape, paper and pen or pencil, a comfortable chair, and as quiet a location as you can. Take the phone off the hook. Record the session written in italics in the **Programming Cycle** section by reading the words out loud and recording them on a cassette tape. Where instructions say PAUSE, stop talking for about three seconds or so while the tape continues to run. Then resume reading the italicized words. For longer pauses, the instructions will say STOP TALKING FOR X SECONDS while letting the tape continue to run. You can either use a watch or just count slowly (silently) to approximate the number of seconds. In place of X, the instructions will specify a number such as 10.

This session requires some additional preparation. You must prepare some written material *before* you listen to the tape recording and perform the exercise. You will need this material during the programming cycle. Take a sheet of paper and draw a large circle on it. A free-hand circle is good enough. If you want to be precise, take a salad plate or bowl and place it upside down on the paper and trace around it. Divide the circle into four approximately equal sections by drawing a line through it from top to bottom and another line across it through the center of the circle. Somewhere on the paper outside the circle write: "Some personal goals for (sign your name) with harm to no one." Then write the date. Then write one personal goal in each of the four sections of the circle.

Be specific in your descriptions. For instance, if you are a bank teller and you want to be promoted to head teller, write "Promotion to head teller at (name of bank)." Don't just write a vague statement like "I want to get ahead." If you are able to express your goal in a picture, so much the better. Either draw a picture or paste a picture in the section of the circle. If you draw, it does not have to be a work of art. (On one of my papers I once drew a childish sketch of many books; under the sketch I wrote, "I want to be a successful author of many books.") Put whatever four goals you want; you will be able to add as many more goals in the future as you wish. For now, to learn the procedure, you will deal with just four. If you have a temporary block and are not able to come up with some goals for this programming cycle, here are some suggested ones to start you thinking:

1. I want to become a good, practicing psychic.

2. I want to successfully overcome (name of some undesirable habit or trait you really want to correct).

3. I want to become a skilled, successful (name of skill).

Put in a picture if you can. For example, if you want to be a successful beautician, cut the picture of a beautician and/or beauty salon from a magazine or newspaper and tape it onto your circle. If the picture is large, just tape a corner of it and then fold it up.

You probably have the idea by now. After you have filled your circle, study it to fix it in your mind; you will need to recall it when in your programming cycle. Then fold the paper and put it in an envelope. This envelope will be your goal keeper.

Programming Cycle: After you have recorded the following instructions (only record the italicized words), rewind the tape. Then relax in your chair, turn your recorder to PLAY, close your eyes and listen to the tape and follow the instructions given on the tape.

Go to your psychic workshop using the 3-2-1 method, followed by descending your psychic staircase while slowly counting from 10 down to 1 on each step down. I will stop talking while you do this. STOP TALKING FOR 60 SECONDS WHILE ALLOWING THE TAPE TO CONTINUE RUNNING. *You are in your psychic workshop now. Settle into a comfortable position in your chair.* PAUSE *Press your control button and allow your psychic chalkboard to descend in front of you.* PAUSE *With a piece of chalk, draw a circle on the board and divide it into four sections just as you did in preparing your goals before this programming cycle.* PAUSE

Now fill in your goals in the circle just as you did on paper prior to this programming cycle. If you had pictures on your paper, just visualize them as you write on your chalkboard. I will stop talking now for two minutes while you complete this. STOP TALKING FOR 2 MINUTES WHILE THE TAPE CONTINUES TO RUN. *Now write on the board "With harm to no one" and sign your name.* STOP TALKING FOR 15 SECONDS WHILE THE TAPE CONTINUES TO RUN.

You now have recorded some personal goals on your psychic chalkboard. You have also previously recorded these goals on paper and placed them in your goal keeper. Now repeat the following words mentally to yourself as I say them: "These are my goals which I now release to my higher mind." *PAUSE Now press your button and allow the chalkboard to raise up out of sight carrying your message to your higher mind. Your goals are now an established fact at the psychic level, and will materialize in the physical realm in the manner and at the time most appropriate for you in accordance with your consciousness, and this is so. PAUSE*

Now it is time for you to establish a motto and a creed to guide you in your psychic practice. PAUSE Press your button to lower your psychic movie screen. PAUSE Press your button again to bring in a slide projector at the right-hand side of your chair. PAUSE This is an automatic projector and is already loaded with the proper slides. PAUSE Press your button. The slide projector clicks and projects on your screen the following words: "My motto is 'Pass It On.' " *PAUSE Read the words to yourself. PAUSE*

Now mentally repeat the words as I say them: "My motto is 'Pass It On.' " *PAUSE This powerful motto is your commitment to yourself and to your higher mind to pass on to others the enrichment and beneficial energies that are channeled through you by your higher mind. You realize that universal law is at work here. The law states that you receive only by giving, and the more you give, the more you receive, enabling you to give even more. It is the universal law of reciprocity. PAUSE Once again repeat,* "My motto is 'Pass It On.' " *Now press your button and the projector flashes another message on your screen. Read the message with me mentally as I say it:* "My creed is:

I shall pass through this world but once.
Any good therefore that I can do,
Or any kindness that I can show
To any human being, let me do it now.
Let me not defer or neglect it
For I shall not pass this way again."

PAUSE

Make a commitment now to yourself to write this creed down after you return to beta, and then memorize it, and then put it in your goal keeper. PAUSE *Press your button once again to turn off your projector and return your movie screen to its place.* PAUSE *You have now established some goals, a motto, and a creed. You are now better equipped to become a practicing psychic and a better citizen of the universe.* PAUSE *Now it is time to return to the ground floor of your skyscraper of consciousness and to beta.* PAUSE *Count yourself out in the usual manner, from 1 to 10 as you climb your staircase, and then the 1 to 5 countout and open your eyes.*

After Programming: Take your pen/pencil and paper and write the following—Session #4 is completed. Write the date. Sign your name. Be sure to use the writing modifications described earlier in this chapter. Then keep your paper as your record of achievement so you do not inadvertently skip a session.

Optional Additional Programming: This is an optional extra to help you tune yourself up even more. Do not substitute this exercise for the main programming cycle listed above. This is just an additional exercise if you want to hone yourself even more. You don't have to perform this optional exercise, but I recommend that you do if you have the extra time available to you. You can gain much if you do perform it, but you will not lose anything if you don't.

Enter your workshop and program any other goals you may want. Follow the same routine as detailed for the main programming cycle. First draw your circle on paper and enter the goals. Then study it to fix it in your mind. Then put the paper in your goal keeper. Then go to your workshop and write it on your blackboard and release it to your higher mind just as in the main programming cycle.

Comments: You can program as many goals or projects as you wish using the method described in today's exercise. There is no limit. If one envelope fills up, start another. You can put as many or as few items on one paper as you wish.

I used photocopy reduction to reduce one of my goal papers to about two inches square so I could carry it in my wallet. I put the original in my goal keeper. Of course, the reduced version is almost unreadable, but I can look at it and instantly know what is on it.

Review your goal keeper once in a while, perhaps once or twice a year, to see how you are doing. You can modify your goals if you wish, using the same procedure as when you created it. For example, suppose you had originally established a goal of being a successful banker. That was really what you believed was your best talent at the time. When you released the goal to your higher mind, some things started to happen. Your higher mind presented you with experiences and greater awareness that showed you that being a tax consultant captured your talents and interest much more than banking. Perhaps over a several-year period, your higher mind leads you in this new direction by clearly showing you other options. The thing to do is remove or cross out the original goal and replace it with the new goal.

Life is not static. It is a constant flow of change as you learn and experience more. The only thing constant in life is change. Those who understand the nature of change welcome it, and learn to use change to their advantage to move ahead in life and enrich their lives. Those who fear change and refuse to accept change move backwards in life and lose their enrichment. There is no such thing as maintaining the status quo insofar as living is concerned. One either moves forward or backward. It is not possible to stay the same.

Your psychic workshop gives you a powerful tool to deal with change and your increased awareness in a beneficial way.

Session #5

Purpose: This session is the last one of those specifically designed to put you into balance and into a proper posture of consciousness so you will be able to become a successful psychic practitioner. This session deals with sending love, removing guilt, sending forgiveness, and fortifying yourself against fear and doubt. You will find that successful psychic practice is dependent on your being in harmony with yourself and with the rest of the world.

Preparation: Get your tape recorder, a blank tape, paper and pen or pencil, a comfortable chair, and as quiet a location as you can. Take the phone off the hook.

Record the session written in italics in the **Programming Cycle** section by reading the words out loud and recording them on a cassette tape. Where instructions say PAUSE, stop talking for about three seconds or so while the tape continues to run. Then resume reading the italicized words. For longer pauses, the instructions will say STOP TALKING FOR X SECONDS while letting the tape continue to run. You can either use a watch or just count slowly (silently) to approximate the number of seconds. In place of X, the instructions will specify a number such as 10.

Programming Cycle: After you have recorded the following instructions (only record the italicized words), rewind the tape. Then relax in your chair, turn your recorder to PLAY, close your eyes and listen to the tape and follow the instructions given on the tape.

Go to your psychic workshop using your 3-2-1 countdown and the 10 to 1 countdown on your staircase. In future exercises you will be simply directed to go to your workshop, and you are to do so using the method you have learned. I will now stop talking for a minute while you go to your workshop and become seated in your chair. STOP TALKING FOR 60 SECONDS WHILE THE TAPE CONTINUES TO RUN.

You are now seated in your chair in your workshop. Press your button and allow the entire wall in front of you to lower into the floor. PAUSE *Beyond the wall is a beautiful white sand beach and a serene, crystal blue ocean. Study this magnificent scene for a moment.* STOP TALKING FOR 10 SECONDS WHILE ALLOWING THE TAPE TO CONTINUE RUNNING.

Now get up and walk forward out onto the nearest edge of the sandy beach. PAUSE *You are on the beach now. The warm sun feels so good. Overhead three seagulls circle looking for food.* PAUSE *Watch their graceful, gliding movement.* PAUSE *Listen to their squawks of communication.* PAUSE *Bend over and remove your shoes and stockings. Leave them here on the sand where you can get them when you return.* PAUSE *Feel the warm, caressing sand against your bare feet.* PAUSE

Now walk forward toward the ocean's edge. PAUSE *You are on wet sand now. Feel its cool firmness under your feet. Notice how different this sand feels compared to the warm, dry sand you were on moments ago.* PAUSE *Look at the majestic expanse of ocean in front of you. It stretches as far as you can see.* PAUSE *A gentle wave comes ashore and rushes past your feet. Feel how it tugs at your ankles as it recedes back to the ocean.* PAUSE *This ocean is the infinite sea of never-ending life and consciousness. Wade out into the water a short distance to where the water comes to your knees.* PAUSE

This sea, of which you are a part, contains all the power you will ever need. Feel the power coming from the ocean floor up through your feet and legs bringing with it love and zest for life.

Bringing with it courage and faith. Stand there and allow this priceless gift from the sea to fill your entire body. Flowing up through your legs. Into the trunk of your body. Flowing into your neck and head. PAUSE *You are filled from the sea of consciousness and life. You feel vibrant with love for life and for all. A powerful peace settles over you.* PAUSE

Courage has filled every facet of your being. You know you can handle anything in a sensible and beneficial manner. You fear nothing at all. You have no fear, and this is so. PAUSE *Tremendous faith races through you. There is no room for doubt, and you have no doubts. You have received faith, courage, power, and zest for life from this infinite source of goodness.* PAUSE

Now walk back to the beach to the point where an occasional wave washes past your ankles. PAUSE *Bend down and write in the wet sand with your finger this message: "I love."* PAUSE *Now under your "I love" message write the names of all those special people in your life to whom you wish to send love. Be sure to include your own name. I will stop talking while you write the names.* STOP TALKING FOR 60 SECONDS WHILE THE TAPE CONTINUES TO RUN. *If you have not yet written your own name, do so quickly.* PAUSE

Now a wave from the sea of consciousness washes up over your message and past your ankles. The wave recedes, washing the beach clean. Your love message has been carried into the sea of universal consciousness where it has become reality. PAUSE *Bend down and write in the wet sand once more. This time write "I forgive" followed by your own name first and then the names of all whom you believe have wronged you in some way. I will give you time now to do this.* STOP TALKING FOR 60 SECONDS WHILE THE TAPE CONTINUES TO RUN. *Now another wave from the sea of infinite consciousness washes over your message and past your ankles. When the wave retreats to the sea it takes with it your message of forgiveness which has now become reality.* PAUSE *You have now purged yourself of guilt, blame, and animosity. You have filled your life with love, courage, faith, and zest. You are in balance and in harmony with all. You are now ready to serve with integrity and success.* PAUSE

Walk back to where your shoes are and put them on. PAUSE *Now walk back to your chair and sit down.* PAUSE *Take one more look at the sea.* PAUSE *The beach.* PAUSE *The seagulls.* PAUSE *Now press your button and allow the end of the room to slide back up into its original position.* PAUSE *Now it is time to return to your conscious level of beta. Return by your usual 1 to 10 countup as you climb the stairs followed by your 1 to 5 countout. In the future you will simply be directed to awaken yourself, and you will do so by this countout method you have learned.*

After Programming: Take your pen/pencil and paper and write the following—Session #5 is completed. Write the date. Sign your name. Be sure to use the writing modifications described earlier in this chapter. Then keep your paper as your record of achievement so you do not inadvertently skip a session.

Optional Additional Programming: This is an optional extra to help you tune yourself up even more. Do not substitute this exercise for the main programming cycle listed above. This is just an additional exercise if you want to hone yourself even more. You don't have to perform this optional exercise, but I recommend that you do if you have the extra time available to you. You can gain much if you do perform it, but you will not lose anything if you don't.

Return to your seashore as in the main programming cycle to add any other names to your list to send love to. You may want to also experience the walk out into the sea of life once again. When finished, awaken yourself in the manner you have been taught.

Comments: Some of you may be physically handicapped in this earth plane and concerned that it is not possi-

ble for you to walk, write, or do any type of physical movement as directed in the programming cycles. Do not be concerned. Physical handicap does not exist in the psychic
realm. Visualize yoursef doing whatever you are directed
to do and it becomes reality at that level of consciousness. In
the psychic world, the only handicap that can exist is one of
restricted imagination, which only you can impose on yourself by allowing yourself to succumb to fear, doubt, or other
negativism. Your psychic world and your psychic abilities
expand or contract with your own imaginative faculties.
Balance, harmony, and other positive energy expand your
imagination and psychic world. Fear, doubt, and other
negative energy contract your imagination and psychic
world. The way you develop is completely your choice. You
alone are responsible for you.

Session #6

Purpose: This session trains your mind for visualizing
shapes and colors, and it sensitizes your psychic center to
smells, taste and touch. This and several subsequent exercises train your mind for future psychic work by establish-
ing psychic reference points.

Preparation: Get your tape recorder, a blank tape,
paper and pen or pencil, a comfortable chair, and as quiet a
location as you can. Take the phone off the hook.

Record the session written in italics in the **Programming Cycle** section by reading the words out loud and
recording them on a cassette tape. Where instructions say
PAUSE, stop talking for about three seconds or so while the
tape continues to run. Then resume reading the italicized
words. For longer pauses, the instructions will say STOP
TALKING FOR X SECONDS while letting the tape continue to run. You can either use a watch or just count slowly

(silently) to approximate the number of seconds. In place of X, the instructions will specify a number such as 10.

During this exercise, and some future exercises, there will be the command SNAP. This means at that point in your recording to snap your fingers. Be sure to snap close enough to the microphone to pick up the sound. This SNAP is used as a signal for you to mentally do certain things. If you are unable to snap your fingers (some people are not able to), then clap your hands once, or click a mechanical clicker, or make a click with your tongue, etc. The idea is to make one distinctive, sharp sound at the point where the instructions say SNAP.

Programming Cycle: After you have recorded the following instructions (only record the italicized words), rewind the tape. Then relax in your chair, turn your recorder to PLAY, close your eyes and listen to the tape, and follow the instructions given on the tape.

Close your eyes and enter your psychic workshop. STOP TALKING FOR 60 SECONDS WHILE THE TAPE CONTINUES TO RUN. *Press your button and bring in a table with a white tablecloth and sit it in front of you.* STOP TALKING FOR 10 SECONDS, TAPE RUNNING. *In a moment I am going to count from 1 to 3 and snap my fingers. When I do, create a green watermelon sitting on your white tablecloth. One. Two. Three. SNAP.*

Observe the green watermelon. PAUSE *Notice the elliptical shape.* PAUSE *Notice the contrast of the green against the white tablecloth.* PAUSE *Feel the cool, smooth skin of the watermelon. You have felt watermelon before. Recall the feeling.* PAUSE *Smell it.* PAUSE *When I snap my fingers the tablecloth will become red. SNAP. PAUSE How does the green melon contrast against the red cloth?* PAUSE *When I snap, the cloth will become orange. SNAP.* PAUSE *Notice the color contrast now.* PAUSE *When I snap, the cloth will be yellow.* SNAP. PAUSE *Observe the color contrast.* PAUSE *When I snap, the cloth will be green.* SNAP. PAUSE *How does the green melon stand out against a green background?* PAUSE

When I snap, the cloth will be blue. SNAP. PAUSE *Observe the colors and contrast.* PAUSE *When I snap, the cloth will be black.* SNAP. PAUSE *Observe the color contrast.* PAUSE *When I snap, the cloth will go back to blue.* SNAP. PAUSE *Now back to green.* SNAP. PAUSE *Back to yellow.* SNAP. PAUSE *Back to orange.* SNAP. PAUSE *Back to red.* SNAP. PAUSE *Back to white.* SNAP. PAUSE

Now when I snap, the watermelon will be cut in half. SNAP. PAUSE *Observe the inside of the melon. Notice the contrast of the tiny black seeds throughout the ruby red fruit.* PAUSE *Scoop out a piece of the red fruit and taste it.* PAUSE *How sweet is it? What does it feel like in your mouth? What is the texture and moisture content? Recall and observe these things and establish them as reference points in your psychic center.* PAUSE

When I snap, the watermelon will disappear. SNAP. PAUSE *Now when I snap, a lemon will appear on the white tablecloth.* SNAP. PAUSE *Observe the lemon.* PAUSE *Its shape.* PAUSE *Its bright yellow color.* PAUSE *Feel the skin.* PAUSE *Notice how the lemon oil in the skin makes it feel silky.* PAUSE *Smell it.* PAUSE *The lemon fragrance is clean and pleasant.* PAUSE *Notice the contrast of the yellow lemon against the white tablecloth.* PAUSE

When I snap, the cloth will be red. SNAP. PAUSE *Observe the color contrast.* PAUSE *When I snap, the cloth will be orange.* SNAP. PAUSE *Observe the color contrast.* PAUSE *When I snap, the cloth will be yellow.* SNAP. PAUSE *How does a yellow lemon contrast against a yellow cloth?* PAUSE *When I snap, the cloth will be green.* SNAP. PAUSE *Observe the contrast now.* PAUSE *When I snap, the cloth will be blue.* SNAP. PAUSE *Observe the colors and the contrast.* PAUSE *When I snap, the cloth will be black.* SNAP. PAUSE *Observe the contrast now.* PAUSE

When I snap, the cloth will go back to blue. SNAP. PAUSE

Now back to green. SNAP. PAUSE Back to yellow. SNAP. PAUSE Back to orange. SNAP. PAUSE Back to red. SNAP. PAUSE Back to white. SNAP. PAUSE Now when I snap, the lemon will be cut in half so you can observe the inside. SNAP. PAUSE Notice the fruit is a lighter yellow than the skin. PAUSE Notice the fragrant aroma from the sliced lemon. PAUSE See the droplets of juice running down from the cut. PAUSE

Taste the fruit now. PAUSE Notice the sour taste that puckers your mouth. PAUSE How does this compare to the taste of the watermelon? PAUSE Recall and observe all these things and establish them as reference points in your psychic center. PAUSE

When I snap, the lemon will disappear. SNAP. PAUSE When I snap, a carrot will appear on the white tablecloth. SNAP. PAUSE Observe the orange carrot with the leafy green top. PAUSE Notice the long, tapered shape of the carrot and the bushy green top. PAUSE Notice the color contrasts against the white tablecloth. PAUSE Feel the carrot. Notice how hard it is. PAUSE Now feel the green top. Notice how soft and fluffy it is. PAUSE Smell the carrot and the carrot top. PAUSE

When I snap, the cloth will be red. SNAP. PAUSE Observe the color contrasts now. PAUSE When I snap the cloth will be orange. SNAP. PAUSE Observe the color contrasts. PAUSE When I snap, the cloth will be yellow. SNAP. PAUSE Observe the color contrasts. PAUSE When I snap, the cloth will be green. SNAP. PAUSE Observe the orange carrot and the green top against a green tablecloth. PAUSE When I snap, the cloth will be blue. SNAP. PAUSE Observe the color contrast now. PAUSE When I snap, the cloth will be black. SNAP. Observe the carrot and top against the black background. PAUSE

When I snap, the cloth will go back to blue. SNAP. Now back to green. SNAP. Now back to yellow. SNAP. Back to orange. SNAP. Back to red. SNAP. Back to white. SNAP. PAUSE Now taste the carrot. Notice how firm and crunchy it is. PAUSE Recall and observe all these things and establish them as reference points in your psychic center. PAUSE

When I snap, the carrot will disappear. SNAP. PAUSE When I snap, a red, ripe tomato will appear on your white tablecloth. SNAP. PAUSE Observe the tomato. PAUSE Notice the round shape. See how the red color contrasts against the white cloth background. PAUSE Feel the tomato. Notice it is somewhat firm but gives to your touch when you press it. PAUSE How does the tomato feel as compared to the carrot? PAUSE How does the skin feel? PAUSE Smell the tomato. PAUSE When I snap, the cloth will be red. SNAP. PAUSE How does the red tomato contrast against the red cloth? PAUSE When I snap, the cloth will be orange. SNAP. PAUSE Observe the colors. PAUSE When I snap, the cloth will be yellow. SNAP. PAUSE What is the color contrast now? PAUSE When I snap, the color of the cloth will be green. SNAP. PAUSE Observe the color contrast. PAUSE When I snap, the cloth will be blue. SNAP. PAUSE Observe the colors. PAUSE When I snap, the cloth will be black. SNAP. PAUSE Observe the color contrast. PAUSE

When I snap, the cloth will go back to blue. SNAP. Back to green. SNAP. Back to yellow. SNAP. Back to orange. SNAP. Back to red. SNAP. Back to white. SNAP. PAUSE When I snap, the tomato will be cut in half so you can observe the inside. SNAP. PAUSE Notice the juice that runs down from the cut. PAUSE Taste the tomato. PAUSE How does the texture compare to the carrot? What does the tomato taste like? PAUSE Recall and observe all these things and establish them as reference points in your psychic center. PAUSE When I snap, the tomato will disappear. SNAP. PAUSE

You have now trained your mind to respond quickly to many changes in shapes, colors, and substances. You have established some valuable reference points in your psychic center that will aid you in your future psychic work. PAUSE

Now it is time to return to the beta level of consciousness. Take yourself back to beta and awaken using the method you have learned.

After Programming: Take your pen/pencil and paper and write the following—Session #6 is completed. Write the date. Sign your name. Be sure to use the writing modifications described earlier in this chapter. Then keep your paper as your record of achievement so you do not inadvertently skip a session.

Optional Additional Programming: This is an optional extra to help you tune yourself up even more. Do not substitute this exercise for the main programming cycle listed above. This is just an additional exercise if you want to hone yourself even more. You don't have to perform this optional exercise, but I recommend that you do if you have the extra time available to you. You can gain much if you do perform it, but you will not lose anything if you don't.

Return to your psychic workshop and perform more examinations of shapes, substances, and colors just as in the main programming cycle. Some suggested items are a purple plum, brown potato, or anything else you wish. Stay as long as you wish in your workshop, and return by your usual method.

Comments: Notice how much more quickly your mind now responds to command, and how much more vivid your imagery is becoming. All your senses are becoming more finely tuned. This fine tuning will continue over the next several sessions in particular, and in fact continues every time you go to your workshop.

Session #7

Purpose: This exercise teaches you to project your intelligence into inanimate objects and retrieve information. This is the first of several exercises that will ultimately teach you to project your intelligence anywhere in the universe. These exercises establish reference points in your psychic center.

Preparation: Get your tape recorder, a blank tape, paper and pen or pencil, a comfortable chair, and as quiet a location as you can. Take the phone off the hook.

Record the session written in italics in the **Programming Cycle** section by reading the words out loud and recording them on a cassette tape. Where instructions say PAUSE, stop talking for about three seconds or so while the tape continues to run. Then resume reading the italicized words. For longer pauses, the instructions will say STOP TALKING FOR X SECONDS while letting the tape continue to run. You can either use a watch or just count slowly (silently) to approximate the number of seconds. In place of X, the instructions will specify a number such as 10.

Before you begin to listen to the tape you have just made, there are several other preparatory things you need to do.

1. Get a piece of wood. Any kind. Any size. If you are having difficulty finding wood, try looking in your kitchen. You can use a wooden spoon or the handle of a knife.

2. Get a piece of stainless steel. The blade of a stainless steel kitchen knife will be fine.

3. Get a cotton ball. You probably have some in your medicine cabinet. Or perhaps in the top of a bottle of vitamins. Or remove the cotton from a cotton swab.

Take a few minutes now before listening to the tape to do the following:

1. Hold the wood in your hands. Feel its texture. Smell the wood. Place the wood against your forehead and close your eyes for about five seconds and sense the wood. You are recording impressions of the wood so that you can use

them in the programming cycle.

2. Hold the stainless steel in your hands. Feel its texture. Smell the stainless steel. Place the stainless steel against your forehead and close your eyes for about five seconds and sense the stainless steel. You are recording impressions of the stainless steel so that you can use them in the programming cycle.

3. Hold the cotton in your hand. Feel its texture. Smell the cotton. Place the cotton against your forehead and close your eyes for about five seconds and sense the cotton. You are recording impressions of the cotton so that you can use them in the programming cycle.

Now lay the wood, the stainless steel, and the cotton a foot or so from you.

Now you can proceed with the programming cycle.

Programming Cycle: After you have recorded the following instructions (only record the italicized words), rewind the tape. Then relax in your chair, turn your recorder to PLAY, close your eyes and listen to the tape and follow the instructions given on the tape.

Go to your psychic workshop. STOP TALKING FOR 30 SECONDS WITH THE TAPE STILL RUNNING. *You are seated in your workshop now. Take a deep breath and relax.* PAUSE *Now visualize the piece of wood that you are using for this exercise.* PAUSE *The piece of wood is lying just a few feet from you.* PAUSE *Examine the wood externally with your intelligence. What color is it? Is it smooth or rough?* PAUSE *In a moment I am going to snap my fingers. When I do, you will be inside the wood just underneath the outside surface.* PAUSE *SNAP.*

You are now just under the outside surface of the wood. PAUSE *What is it like in here?* PAUSE *Is the molecular structure dense or roomy?* PAUSE *Notice the light qualities and color.*

PAUSE *What is the temperature? Cool? Warm? Very warm?* PAUSE *Now when I snap my fingers you will be in the center of the wood.* SNAP. *You are now in the center of the wood.* PAUSE *Now what is it like? Is it any different than the outside edge?* PAUSE *Observe color, texture, light, molecular structure, temperature.* STOP TALKING FOR 10 SECONDS WITH TAPE STILL RUNNING.

What do you see? PAUSE *What do you feel?* PAUSE *What do you hear?* PAUSE *All these things are recorded now in your psychic center for future use.* PAUSE *Now when I snap my fingers, you will be back again to the outside edge of the wood.* SNAP. *Now back into your chair.* SNAP. PAUSE

Now visualize the stainless steel that you are using for this exercise. PAUSE *The stainless steel is lying just a few feet from you.* PAUSE *Examine the stainless steel externally with your intelligence. What color is it? Is it smooth or rough?* PAUSE *In a moment I am going to snap my fingers. When I do, you will be inside the steel just underneath the outside surface.* PAUSE SNAP.

You are now just under the outside surface of the stainless steel. PAUSE *What is it like in here?* PAUSE *Is the molecular structure dense or roomy?* PAUSE *Notice the light qualities and color.* PAUSE *What is the temperature? Cool? Warm? Very warm?* PAUSE *Now when I snap my fingers you will be in the center of the stainless steel.* SNAP. *You are now in the center of the stainless steel.* PAUSE *Now what is it like? Is it different than the outside edge?* PAUSE *Observe color, texture, light, molecular structure, temperature.* STOP TALKING FOR 10 SECONDS WHILE TAPE CONTINUES RUNNING.

What do you see? PAUSE *What do you feel?* PAUSE *What do you hear?* PAUSE *How does the stainless steel compare to the wood?* PAUSE *All these things are recorded now in your psychic center for future use.* PAUSE *Now when I snap my fingers you will be back again to the outside edge of the stainless steel.* SNAP. *Now back into your chair.* PAUSE

Now visualize the piece of cotton that you are using for this exercise. PAUSE *The piece of cotton is lying just a few feet from you.* PAUSE *Examine the cotton externally with your intelligence. What color is is? Is it smooth or rough?* PAUSE *In a moment I am going to snap my fingers. When I do, you will be inside the cotton just underneath the outside surface.* PAUSE *SNAP.*

You are now just under the outside surface of the cotton. PAUSE *What is it like in here?* PAUSE *Is the molecular structure dense or roomy?* PAUSE *Notice the light qualities and color.* PAUSE *What is the temperature? Cool? Warm? Very warm?* PAUSE *Now when I snap my fingers you will be in the center of the cotton. SNAP. You are now in the center of the cotton.* PAUSE *Now what is it like? Is it any different than the outside edge?* PAUSE *Observe color, texture, light, molecular structure, temperature.* STOP TALKING FOR 10 SECONDS WHILE TAPE CONTINUES RUNNING.

What do you see? PAUSE *What do you feel?* PAUSE *What do you hear?* PAUSE *How does the cotton compare to the steel and to the wood?* PAUSE *All these things are recorded now in your psychic center for future use.* PAUSE *Now when I snap my fingers you will be back again to the outside edge of the cotton. SNAP. Now back into your chair. SNAP.* PAUSE

You are now learning to project your intelligence and to sense, see, feel, and hear what is happening at the point to which you projected. PAUSE *In the next session you will experience projecting into plant life.* PAUSE *Every time you project your intelligence, you add to your knowledge, increase your psychic awareness, and enhance your ability to function as a practicing psychic, and this is so.* PAUSE *Now it is time to return to beta. Exit your workshop and open your eyes.*

After Programming: Take your pen/pencil and paper and write the following—Session #7 is completed. Write the date. Sign your name. Be sure to use the writing modifications described earlier in this chapter. Then keep your paper as your record of achievement so you do not inadvertently skip a session.

Optional Additional Programming: This is an optional extra to help you tune yourself up even more. Do not substitute this exercise for the main programming cycle listed above. This is just an additional exercise if you want to hone yourself even more. You don't have to perform this optional exercise, but I recommend that you do if you have the extra time available to you. You can gain much if you do perform it, but you will not lose anything if you don't.

Do the same procedure as given for the main programming cycle, except use different inanimate objects. Some suggestions: your wall, a sheet of paper, a statue, a glass object, a piece of any kind of metal (except stainless steel, which you have already done), etc.

Comments: Mental projection is a major part of psychic work. Practice and learn it well. By the time you finish these 30 sessions you will be well versed in mental projection.

Session #8

Purpose: In this session you will experience projecting into nonintelligent living matter by projecting into plant life. This is further enhancement of your psychic ability.

Preparation: Get your tape recorder, a blank tape, paper and pen or pencil, a comfortable chair, and as quiet a location as you can. Take the phone off the hook.

Record the session written in italics in the **Programming Cycle** section by reading the words out loud and recording them on a cassette tape. Where instructions say PAUSE, stop talking for about three seconds or so while the tape continues to run. Then resume reading the italicized words. For longer pauses, the instructions will say STOP TALKING FOR X SECONDS while letting the tape continue to run. You can either use a watch or just count slowly (silently) to approximate the number of seconds. In place of X, the instructions will specify a number such as 10.

You will need a plant that has leaves, a stem, and roots. Any kind of plant that meets those requirements will do just fine. For this initial exercise, do not use a plant like a cactus that has no leaves, or a dandelion that has no stem; you may use these in your optional additional programming if you wish.

If you have a house plant, bring it to where you will be performing your exercise if you can. If you do not have a plant, go outside and select a tree, a plant or a weed (do not dig it up) and that will be your plant for this exercise.

Take a few moments to do the following with your selected plant before you do your programming cycle.

1. Touch a leaf. Stroke it. Feel its texture. Smell it. Study its shape, color, and appearance. Press the leaf gently to your forehead (if possible) and close your eyes for a few seconds to record impressions.
2. Touch the stem. Stroke it. Feel its texture. Smell it. Study its shape, color and appearance.
3. Imagine what the roots might be like. Color. Texture. Odor. Appearance.

Programming Cycle: After you have recorded the following instructions (only record the italicized words), rewind the tape. Then relax in your chair, turn your recorder to PLAY, close your eyes and listen to the tape and follow the instructions given on the tape.

Go to your psychic workshop. STOP TALKING FOR 25 SECONDS WHILE TAPE CONTINUES RUNNING. *You are seated in your workshop now. Take a deep breath and relax.*

PAUSE *Now visualize the plant that you are using for this exercise.* PAUSE *Examine the plant externally with your intelligence.* PAUSE *Notice the leaf shape and density. Notice the stem thickness and length. Observe the colors.* PAUSE *In a moment, when I snap my fingers, project your intelligence into the center of the leaf.* SNAP. *You are now in the center of the leaf.* PAUSE *What is it like in here?* PAUSE *Is the molecular structure dense or roomy?* PAUSE *Notice the light quality and color.* PAUSE *What is the temperature like?* PAUSE *What is the internal structure of this leaf?* PAUSE

How does living matter compare to the inanimate matter you have previously investigated? PAUSE *Is there any sort of movement inside this leaf?* PAUSE *What do you see?* PAUSE *What do you feel?* PAUSE *What do you sense?* PAUSE *What do you hear?* PAUSE *Take some time to observe color, texture, light, structure, temperature, movement, sounds, and so forth.* STOP TALKING FOR 15 SECONDS WHILE THE TAPE CONTINUES RUNNING. *All these things are recorded now in your psychic center for future use.* PAUSE

Now when I snap my fingers, you will be inside the center of the main stem of the plant. SNAP. PAUSE *You are now in the center of the stem.* PAUSE *What is it like in here?* PAUSE *Is the molecular structure dense or roomy?* PAUSE *Notice the light quality and color.* PAUSE *What is the temperature like?* PAUSE

What is the internal structure of this stem? PAUSE *How does the stem compare to the leaf you have just investigated?* PAUSE *Is there any sort of movement inside this stem?* PAUSE *What do you see?* PAUSE *What do you feel?* PAUSE *What do you sense?* PAUSE *What do you hear?* PAUSE *Take some time to observe color, texture, light, structure, temperature, movement, sounds, and so forth.* STOP TALKING FOR 15 SECONDS WHILE TAPE CONTINUES RUNNING. *All these things are recorded now in your psychic center for future use.* PAUSE *Now when I snap my fingers, you will be at the outside edge of the main stem.* SNAP. PAUSE

You are now at the outside edge of the main stem. How does this compare to the center of the stem? PAUSE *Is the light any different?* PAUSE *Take some time to observe color, texture, light, structure, temperature, movement, sounds, and so forth.* STOP TALKING FOR 15 SECONDS WHILE TAPE CONTINUES RUNNING. *How does the outer edge of the stem compare with the center of the stem?* PAUSE *All these things are recorded now in your psychic center for future use.* PAUSE

Now when I snap my fingers, you will be in the center of the plant's main root. SNAP. PAUSE *You are now in the center of the main root.* PAUSE *What is it like in here?* PAUSE *Is the molecular structure dense or roomy?* PAUSE *Notice the light quality and color.* PAUSE *What is the temperature like?* PAUSE *What is the internal structure of this root?* PAUSE *How does this root compare to the stem and the leaf you previously investigated?* PAUSE

Is there any sort of movement inside this root? PAUSE *What do you see?* PAUSE *What do you feel?* PAUSE *What do you sense?* PAUSE *What do you hear?* PAUSE *Take some time to observe color, texture, light, structure, temperature, movement, sounds and so forth.* STOP TALKING FOR 15 SECONDS WHILE THE TAPE CONTINUES RUNNING. *All these things are recorded now in your psychic center for future use.* PAUSE *Now when I snap my fingers, you will be outside the plant.* SNAP. *Now back into your chair.* SNAP. PAUSE

You have enhanced your ability to project your intelligence and to sense, see, feel, and hear what is happening at the point to which you projected. PAUSE *In the next session you will experience projecting into intelligent animal life.* PAUSE *Every time you project your intelligence you add to your knowledge, increase your psychic awareness, and enhance your ability to function as a practicing psychic, and this is so.* PAUSE *Now you may leave your workshop and open your eyes.*

After Programming: Take your pen/pencil and paper and write the following—Session #8 is completed. Write

the date. Sign your name. Be sure to use the writing modifications described earlier in this chapter. Then keep your paper as your record of achievement so you do not inadvertently skip a session.

Optional Additional Programming: This is an optional extra to help you tune yourself up even more. Do not substitute this exercise for the main programming cycle listed above. This is just an additional exercise if you want to hone yourself even more. You don't have to perform this optional exercise, but I do recommend that you do if you have the extra time available to you. You can gain much if you do perform it, but you will not lose anything if you don't.

Go to your psychic workshop and project into a different plant and examine it just as you did in the main programming cycle. You can do this as often as you wish with as many plants as you wish. You might find it interesting to project into a cactus.

Comments: You are rapidly building up experiences at a psychic level. These exercises are extremely important because they train your mind to respond to what you want. Your mind has unlimited capability, but it must be trained and made to focus on a task. The next session will be even more exciting because you will be entering intelligent animal life and exploring it in depth.

Session #9

Purpose: In this session you will experience projecting into intelligent living animal life. This is a significant enhancement of your psychic abilities.

Preparation: Get your tape recorder, a blank tape, paper and pen or pencil, a comfortable chair, and as quiet a location as you can. Take the phone off the hook.

Record the session written in italics in the **Programming Cycle** section by reading the words out loud and recording them on a cassette tape. Where instructions say PAUSE, stop talking for about three seconds or so while the tape continues to run. Then resume reading the italicized words. For longer pauses, the instructions will say STOP TALKING FOR X SECONDS while letting the tape continue to run. You can either use a watch or just count slowly (silently) to approximate the number of seconds. In place of X, the instructions will specify a number such as 10.

You will need a living animal for this exercise. The animal does not need to be physically present because you will not be physically in contact with it as you were for the plant life exercise. For this exercise, the word animal means any living creature: mammals, birds, rodents, reptiles, fish, etc. Take a few moments to select the creature you wish to use. If you have a pet, use it. Or use a friend's pet. Or use some animal you know about such as some famous animal. The only requirement is that it be a specific, living creature (not a deceased one). It is not sufficient to decide to use a "dog." It must be a specific dog such as "my son's collie named Lad."

In this programming cycle, the animal you select will just be referred to as "your pet" because only you know the identity of the animal you have selected. When you have made your selection, think about the animal for a few moments, and then listen to the tape you have made for this training exercise.

Programming Cycle: After you have recorded the following instructions (only record the italicized words), rewind the tape. Then relax in your chair, turn your recorder to PLAY, close your eyes and listen to the tape and follow the instructions given on the tape.

Go to your psychic workshop. STOP TALKING FOR 25 SECONDS WHILE THE TAPE CONTINUES RUNNING. *You are seated in your workshop now. Take a deep breath and relax.* PAUSE *It is time to invite your pet into your workshop. Call out the pet's identity and invite it to enter. Press your control button to open the door so your pet can enter.* STOP TALKING FOR 5 SECONDS WHILE THE TAPE CONTINUES RUNNING.

Your pet has entered and is in front of you. PAUSE *Study it. Observe the physical structure. The colors. The movement. The sounds.* STOP TALKING FOR 10 SECONDS WHILE THE TAPE CONTINUES RUNNING. *Call your pet to come to you.* PAUSE *Observe its movement.* PAUSE *Touch and stroke it. How does it feel?* PAUSE *Have it return to its place.* PAUSE *Again observe the movement.* PAUSE *In a moment, I am going to snap my fingers. When I do, your awareness will be projected inside your pet's brain.* SNAP.

You are now inside your pet's brain. PAUSE *What does it look like in there?* PAUSE *What does it feel like?* PAUSE *Is there any movement?* PAUSE *Any sounds?* PAUSE *Sense your pet's mental processes.* PAUSE *Is it thinking?* PAUSE *Take your time and thoroughly examine all these things in your pet's brain. Observe everything. Nerves. Cells. Blood. Tissue. You have ninety seconds to do this.* STOP TALKING FOR 90 SECONDS WHILE THE TAPE CONTINUES RUNNING.

Did everything appear normal and healthy? PAUSE *If you detected anything that did not appear to be normal and healthy, go back and fix it now, using whatever you need from your psychic medicine chest.* STOP TALKING FOR 30 SECONDS WHILE THE TAPE CONTINUES RUNNING. *Now when I snap my fingers, you will be in your pet's skeleton in the skull bone.* SNAP. PAUSE

What is the bone structure like? PAUSE *How do bone cells compare to the brain cells?* PAUSE *Now allow your intelligence to scan the entire skeleton of your pet, observing everything as you go. If you see broken or cracked bones or other abnormalities, fix*

them immediately before going further. You have ninety seconds to do this. STOP TALKING FOR 90 SECONDS WHILE THE TAPE CONTINUES RUNNING.

When I snap my fingers, project your intelligence into your pet's bloodstream. SNAP. PAUSE

You have entered your pet's bloodstream. What is the color of the blood? PAUSE Allow yourself to be carried through the entire blood circulation system while you observe everything. Cell structure and color. Nutrients. If you detect any abnormalities, fix them immediately. You have ninety seconds to explore the blood system. STOP TALKING FOR 90 SECONDS WHILE THE TAPE CONTINUES RUNNING.

When I snap my fingers, project your intelligence into your pet's heart. SNAP. You are now in your pet's heart. Look around. STOP TALKING FOR 6 SECONDS WITH TAPE STILL RUNNING. *What do you see? PAUSE What do you feel? PAUSE What do you sense? PAUSE What do you hear? PAUSE Is the heart a healthy color? PAUSE Is the heart the normal size, neither enlarged nor shriveled? PAUSE If you detect any abnormality, correct it.* STOP TALKING FOR 10 SECONDS WITH TAPE RUNNING.

Notice the heart rhythm and beat. Watch the heart valves open and close as the heart circulates the blood. PAUSE Take your time and examine the heart thoroughly, and correct any abnormalities that you may detect. STOP TALKING FOR 60 SECONDS WITH TAPE RUNNING.

Now when I snap my fingers, project your intelligence to slowly scan your pet repeatedly from one end to the other internally and externally. Notice all the vital organs. Pay attention to colors and tones. Look for any signs of abnormal swelling or discoloration. Look for signs of disease. Examine muscle and tissue. Look carefully at the skin. Examine the respiratory system. Examine the digestive system. Take your time. Correct any abnormalities if you should encounter any. You have three minutes. STOP TALKING FOR 180 SECONDS WHILE THE TAPE CONTINUES

RUNNING.

You have now experienced an examination of intelligent animal life with your intelligence at a psychic level. All these things are now recorded in your psychic center for future use. PAUSE *Every time you use your psychic ability, you gain knowledge, enhance your psychic ability, and increase your awareness and accuracy, and this is so.* PAUSE *In the next session you will have the first of many experiences exploring a living human body.* PAUSE *Now send love to your pet and then return to beta and open your eyes, using the method you have learned.*

After Programming: Take your pen/pencil and paper and write the following—Session #9 is completed. Write the date. Sign your name. Be sure to use the writing modifications described earlier in this chapter. Then keep your paper as your record of achievement so you do not inadvertently skip a session.

Optional Additional Programming: This is an optional extra to help you tune yourself up even more. Do not substitute this exercise for the main programming cycle listed above. This is just an additional exercise if you want to hone yourself even more. You do not have to perform this optional exercise, but I recommend that you do if you have the extra time available to you. You can gain much if you do perform it, but you will not lose anything if you don't.

Do a repeat of the main programming cycle using a different pet.

Comments: In this session you were directed to correct any abnormalities that you may detect. There were some references to abnormalities and correction of them in some of the Chapter 4 case histories. Otherwise, you have not been specifically instructed concerning abnormalities and correction. This was a deliberate omission.

I wanted you to experience this exercise with as little preconditioning as possible so you could test your own senses and ingenuity in a real situation. Your own psychic center will furnish you the information you need in the way that you can best understand it.

Now let's back up and discuss abnormalities and correction. First, what do healthy body parts look like? You have seen virtually every part of an animal either in the supermarket or in pictures. This is what healthy parts look like. Human organs, tissue, skin, etc., look remarkably similar to the animal counterparts.

Abnormalities will appear psychically as some significant deviation from normal. Color may be different. A blocked heart valve may cause the heart to appear black instead of its normal red color. A diseased organ may seem to have holes in it, be badly deformed, or have strange coloring such as yellow spots on the liver. Abnormality may appear as a swelling or as a withering like a dried prune. You may see scars, growths, or lumps. Or you may see the abnormality as a flashing light. Your own psychic center has its own way of alerting you. When you psychically encounter an abnormality you will know it without question. This does not mean that what you see psychically is an exact replica of what is wrong physically. It may be an exact replica or it may not be. You may detect a diseased organ as having holes in it, but the actual organ (when examined by a physician) may have had tumorous growths on it. In other words, our psychic impression was correct . . . the organ was diseased . . . but your mental image was not literally a replica of the disease.

Whenever you psychically detect an abnormality, immediately correct it psychically. How? There are no limits as to how. The case histories in Chapter 4 give some examples. You may simply remove the defective part and replace it with a perfect part. Your psychic workshop has everything in it you will ever need to correct any problem.

Occasionally you will psychically examine a person who has already had some part removed. Most psychics I know always see the missing part, but it appears different. In my case, I had three such experiences. All three of these were people I had never met. I was working on their cases at the request of concerned friends or family members. In one, I saw the young man's right eye glow as though lighted. I asked my higher mind, "What is this?" I instantly was given the awareness that the person had an artificial right eye. This was confirmed to me by the friend.

In another case, I saw a dotted outline where the gall bladder should have been. Again I asked, "What is this?" I was made aware that the gall bladder was missing due to surgery. This was confirmed to me.

In the third case, I saw a leg that appeared faded while the other leg appeared bold. Again I was given the awareness that the faded leg had been lost in an accident which was later confirmed to me.

When you do psychic readings, use questioning freely to obtain information. In some later sessions you will be given some additional aids and information sources to help you.

In the next session you will explore your first of many human bodies . . . your own body. You do your own body first for two reasons. First, it is the one you are most familiar with, and it will help you establish accurate reference points for future psychic work. Second, it gives you the opportunity to correct any abnormalities and put your own body into better balance. The more in balance you are at every level of self, the better equipped you are to be a good practicing psychic.

If you feel the need, you may want to review the human anatomy in advance of the next session. If you do not have any pictures or books, go to the library. You don't need an in-depth study. Just review in your mind what is in the human body and its approximate locations.

Session #10

Purpose: In this session you will experience psychic investigation of a human body. You will investigate your own body to give you basic training and to help put yourself more in balance.

Preparation: Get your tape recorder, a blank tape, paper and pen or pencil, a comfortable chair, and as quiet a location as you can. Take the phone off the hook.

Record the session written in italics in the **Programming Cycle** section by reading the words out loud and recording them on cassette tape. Where instructions say PAUSE, stop talking for about three seconds or so while the tape continues to run. Then resume reading the italicized words. For longer pauses, the instructions will say STOP TALKING FOR X SECONDS while letting the tape continue to run. You can either use a watch or just count slowly (silently) to approximate the number of seconds. In place of X, the instructions will specify a number such as 10.

Programming Cycle: After you have recorded the following instructions (only record the italicized words), rewind the tape. Then relax in your chair, turn your recorder to PLAY, close your eyes and listen to the tape and follow the instructions given on the tape.

Go to your psychic workshop. STOP TALKING FOR 25 SECONDS WITH THE TAPE CONTINUING TO RUN. *You are in your chair now. Take a deep breath and relax.* PAUSE *In a few moments you are going to scan your body externally and internally with your psychic intelligence. You will have the opportunity to correct any abnormalities if you should encounter any. This exercise will train you for doing psychic work with other people. You will examine your own body by projecting it forward about two feet in front of your intelligence so your intelligence can observe it.* PAUSE

When I snap my fingers, project your body in front of you so you can see it and examine it. SNAP. PAUSE See your body standing in front of you now. PAUSE Have your body face you and remove any clothing if it has any on. PAUSE Start scanning the skin of your body starting at your head and moving down to your toes. Pay particular attention to skin tone, scars, swelling, lumps, burns, extra flab, bruises. If you notice an abnormality, correct it. If you see flab you wish to eliminate, do it. You have a minute to scan and repair, if necessary, the front of your body skin. STOP TALKING FOR 60 SECONDS WHILE THE TAPE CONTINUES RUNNING.

Now when I snap my fingers, have your body turn around so you can examine the rear skin. SNAP. PAUSE You are now observing your body's rear exterior. PAUSE In a moment, when I snap my fingers, begin scanning your back skin from head to foot just as you did for the front skin. Correct any abnormalities if you see any. You have one minute to do this. SNAP. STOP TALKING FOR 60 SECONDS WHILE THE TAPE CONTINUES RUNNING.

Now when I snap my fingers have your body walk away from you for five steps and stop. Observe the walk. SNAP. STOP TALKING FOR 6 SECONDS. *Now when I snap my fingers have your body turn around and walk five steps back toward you and stop. Observe the motion. SNAP.* STOP TALKING FOR 6 SECONDS.

In a few moments I am going to direct you to perform an unusual and extremely beneficial exercise. I am going to ask you to physically reach out with both hands and lift the head off your body in front of you and to bring it back and place it over your head

where you are sitting. This is not harmful in any way because you are superimposing an energy configuration over another energy configuration. The actual physical body is not affected.

In the future you will experience doing this with other people's heads. That is, you will place their head onto yours. This allows you to sense their emotions, thought processes, fears, personality, character, and so forth. This is a very important psychic investigative tool. In this exercise you will be practicing with your own head so you may not experience anything you are not already aware of. PAUSE

Now when I snap my fingers, physically reach out with your hands and lift the head from your body in front of you and bring it back and place it onto your head. SNAP. PAUSE Experience the feeling of the superimposed head. Sense the emotions . . . the thought processes . . . ask any questions of yourself that you wish. STOP TALKING FOR 10 SECONDS. *In the future you can use this technique to explore the emotions, thoughts, fears, character, and personality of other people. PAUSE Now when I snap my fingers, physically reach up and remove the superimposed head and return it to the body in front of you. SNAP. PAUSE Now you are ready to investigate your entire body internally. PAUSE*

When I snap my fingers, project your intelligence into your skeletal structure in the skull. SNAP. PAUSE Now slowly scan all your bones with your intelligence from head to toe. If you notice any abnormality, correct it. Pay attention to joints for burrs or excess calcification build-up. Sand the joints smooth and lubricate them. Put your skeletal structure into first-class shape. Be thorough. You have two minutes. STOP TALKING FOR 120 SECONDS. *Now when I snap my fingers, project your intelligence into your head. SNAP. PAUSE*

Examine everything in your head—your teeth, eyes, brain, ears, cells, nerves, blood flow, glands. Notice colors, movements. If you detect an abnormality, correct it. Be as thorough as you can. You have two minutes. STOP TALKING FOR 120 SECONDS. *Now project into your chest and body trunk. SNAP. PAUSE*

Examine your heart, lungs, liver, stomach, bladder, kidneys, pancreas, sex glands. Notice color, movement, nerves, cells, everything. If you detect an abnormality, correct it. Be thorough. You have three minutes. STOP TALKING FOR 180 SECONDS.

Now when I snap my fingers, begin exploring anything you have not yet investigated. Your throat, arms, hands, legs, feet, blood system. If you detect an abnormality, correct it. Be thorough. You have two minutes. SNAP. STOP TALKING FOR 120 SECONDS.

Now when I snap, return to your chest. SNAP. Now to your head. SNAP. To your skeleton. SNAP. Back to sitting in your chair. SNAP. PAUSE

Now your body in front of you returns to its owner. SNAP. PAUSE

All these things you have experienced are now part of your psychic center for future use. You can psychically investigate your own body whenever you wish in whole or in part and psychically correct any abnormality you may encounter. PAUSE

Every time you enter your psychic workshop you add to your knowledge, enhance your psychic ability, and achieve even greater awareness, and this is so. PAUSE

Now you may leave your workshop and open your eyes using the procedure you have learned.

After Programming: Take your pen/pencil and paper and write the following—Session #10 is completed. Write the date. Sign your name. Be sure to use the writing modifications described earlier in this chapter. Then keep your paper as your record of achievement so you do not inadvertently skip a session.

Optional Additional Programming: If you wish you can record the following instructions and execute them just as you did for the main programming cycle. This is an optional extra to help you tune yourself up even more. Do not substitute this exercise for the main programming cycle listed above. This is just an additional exercise if you want to hone yourself even more. You do not have to perform this optional exercise, but I do recommend that you do if you have the extra time available to you. You can gain much if you do perform it, but you will not lose anything if you don't.

This optional extra is a simple little memory enhancement exercise where you impress on your memory three nearly useless tidbits of trivia. The most difficult things to remember are those things that are not important to you. That is why three unimportant facts have been chosen for you to remember.

Go to your psychic workshop. STOP TALKING FOR 25 SECONDS. *Press your control button and lower your blackboard into place in front of you.* STOP TALKING FOR 5 SECONDS. *Take a piece of chalk and write on your blackboard: "Millard Fillmore was the 13th President of the United States." The spelling is M-I-L-L-A-R-D F-I-L-L-M-O-R-E. Mentally say it as you write it: "Millard Fillmore was the 13th President of the United States."* PAUSE *Now reread to yourself what you wrote.* STOP TALKING FOR 6 SECONDS. *Now press your control button and raise your blackboard up to release the information to your higher mind.* PAUSE *You will always remember now that Millard Fillmore was the 13th President of the United States, and this is so.* PAUSE

Now press your control button and once again lower your blackboard. STOP TALKING FOR 5 SECONDS. *It is once again clean and ready for use.* PAUSE *Write on your blackboard: "George Washington had wooden false teeth."* PAUSE *Mentally say it as you write it: "George Washington had wooden false teeth."* PAUSE *Now reread to yourself what you wrote.* STOP TALKING FOR 6 SECONDS. *Now press your control button and raise your blackboard up to release the information to your higher mind. PAUSE You will always remember now that George Washington had wooden false teeth, and this is so. PAUSE*

Now press your control button and once again lower your blackboard. STOP TALKING FOR 5 SECONDS. *It is once again clean and ready for use. PAUSE Write on your blackboard: "President Grant's middle name is Simpson." Grant's middle name is spelled S-I-M-P-S-O-N. Mentally say it as you write it: President Grant's middle name is Simpson. PAUSE Now reread to yourself what you wrote.* STOP TALKING FOR 6 SECONDS. *Now press your control button and raise your blackboard up to release the information to your higher mind. PAUSE You will always remember now that President Grant's middle name is Simpson, and this is so. PAUSE*

You have now learned one method of remembering items. You will always remember that Millard Fillmore was the 13th President of the United States, that George Washington had wooden false teeth, and that President Grant's middle name is Simpson. PAUSE

You may now exit your psychic workshop and open your eyes. Follow the method you have learned.

Comments: When you become a practicing psychic, much of your work will likely be with people. You will either be giving psychic readings, giving help through psychic healing, helping them put their lives into balance, etc. That is why this session is so important. You will be projecting to other people's bodies several times during the remainder of this 30-session program. However, for the next several sessions you will be doing some other training to more finely tune your psychic ability. Do not start projecting to others until you have had the training for it. This is serious business, and you don't want to act in haste.

One of the most valuable techniques you learned in this session was that of putting on someone's head so you can sense their emotions, mental processes, and thought patterns. In this session, of course, you put on your own head for practice, and I am sure you did not experience any surprises. However, when you put on someone else's head you may find some surprises. I have felt someone else's overpowering fear using this technique. Then I was better able to help them conquer that fear.

Session #11

Purpose: In this session you will project to some places you are already familiar with. While there you will record what you see, feel, sense, and hear. This gives you experience in verbalizing your psychic impressions. As a practicing psychic, you will often need to speak out loud while still in your psychic workshop performing some sort of investigation. In this session you train by visiting places you are familiar with. Future exercises will be projections to places you have never visited. As a practicing psychic, you will frequently be dealing with people, places, or things that you were not previously familiar with.

Preparation: Get your tape recorder, a blank tape, paper and pen or pencil, a comfortable chair, and as quiet a location as you can. Take the phone off the hook.

There are no prerecorded instructions for this exercise. Just put your recorder on RECORD and then go to your workshop and talk.

Programming Cycle: You will not be instructed by a tape recording in this session. You will need to instruct yourself. You are to use your recorder to record what you say while in your psychic workshop. Follow this general procedure:

1. Go to your psychic workshop.
2. Project to your bedroom. Examine your bedroom in detail, speaking out loud as you do. Tell what you are

examining. Give detail. Describe colors, floors, walls, fixtures, lamps, bed covers, furniture, items on the furniture, items on the walls. Say out loud what you see, feel, sense, and hear. Strive for thoroughness and detail.

3. Then project to your bathroom and do the same sort of thing you did in your bedroom. Speak out loud. Strive for thoroughness and detail.
4. Leave your psychic workshop and awaken.
5. Be sure to do your handwriting exercise.
6. Listen to the recording you made. Check your accuracy against what the bedroom and bathroom are like.

After Programming: Take your pen/pencil and paper and write the following—Session #11 is completed. Write the date. Sign your name. Be sure to use the writing modifications described earlier in this chapter. Then keep your paper as your record of achievement so you do not inadvertently skip a session.

Optional Additional Programming: This is an optional extra to help you tune yourself up even more. Do not substitute this exercise for the main programming cycle listed above. This is just an additional exercise if you want to hone yourself even more. You do not have to perform this optional exercise, but I do recommend that you do if you have the extra time available to you. You can gain much if you do perform it, but you do not lose anything if you don't.

Select other places you are familiar with, such as your office, living room, garage, etc., and investigate them. Record verbally what is happening just as you did in the main programming cycle.

Comments: You probably can see a pattern emerging

in your psychic training. You started with simple relaxation, went to some self-balancing and actualization, then began projecting with experiences that you already had some familiarity with, and you will go on to dealing with things which you have had no familiarity with.

You started by being directed word by word, then to being left partly on your own, and finally you will go on to being totally on your own.

You started in silence, just getting mental impressions. Now you are starting to verbalize those impressions.

The building-block fashion of training should now be clear to you.

When you complete your 30-session training, you will be able to go anywhere and do anything completely on your own and be able to tell someone (or a recorder) exactly what is happening while you do it.

Session #12

Purpose: In this session you will experience projecting your awareness to a specific point in the United States where you most likely have never been. While there you will collect information which can then be verified. Even if you have been to the point in question, it is likely that you are not consciously aware of what is there in any detail.

The exercise has two parts. In the first part, you will go to a specific point and will be told what is there. This helps you sensitize your psychic awareness and establish reference points in your mind.

In the second part, you will go to another specific point but will not be told what is there. You will verbally record what you see, sense, feel , and hear there. Then you will be able to match your impressions against what is there; I have written what is at this point in the **Comments** section of this session's exercise.

Preparation: Get your tape recorder, a blank tape, paper and pen or pencil, a comfortable chair, and as quiet a location as you can. Take the phone off the hook.

Record the session written in italics in the **Programming Cycle** section by reading the words out loud and recording them on a cassette tape. Where instructions say PAUSE, stop talking for about three seconds or so while the tape continues to run. Then resume reading the italicized words. For longer pauses, the instructions will say STOP TALKING FOR X SECONDS while letting the tape continue to run. You can either use a watch or just count slowly (silently) to approximate the number of seconds. In place of X, the instructions will specify a number such as 10.

Programming Cycle: After you have recorded the following instructions (only record the italicized words), rewind the tape. Then relax in your chair, turn your recorder to PLAY, close your eyes and listen to the tape and follow the instructions given on the tape.

Go to your psychic workshop. STOP TALKING FOR 25 SECONDS. *You are in your psychic workshop and seated in your chair.* PAUSE *Take a deep breath and relax.* PAUSE *When I snap my fingers, project your awareness to the center of the intersection of Garrison Street and Alameda Avenue in Lakewood, Colorado.* SNAP. PAUSE *You are now in the center of the intersection of Garrison and Alameda in Lakewood, Colorado. Turn and face north.* PAUSE *Do not be concerned about traffic. You are there at a psychic level and cannot be harmed by vehicles.* PAUSE

Allow all your senses to be sharp and sensitive. See, sense, feel, and hear what is at this location. As you face north, you are looking northward on Garrison Street, which is a two-lane blacktop city street. PAUSE *On a diagonal to your left is the northwest corner of this intersection. On this corner is a Pester gas station which can be accessed only from Garrison Street. Sitting to the rear* of the gas station is a small complex of offices in a one-story brick building. These offices all house a cable television company. PAUSE

On a diagonal to your right is the northeast corner of this intersection. On this corner is a small restaurant and lounge with an adjacent liquor store. There is access to the parking lot from both streets. To the east of the liquor store is the Mile High Church of Religious Science. The church is a white, round, domed cement structure. It has a large parking lot with an entrance on Garrison Street just beyond the restaurant. PAUSE

Now turn ninety degrees to your right to face eastward on Alameda Avenue. Alameda is a four-lane blacktop city street. PAUSE Now turn ninety degrees to your right again to face southward on Garrison, a two-lane blacktop city street. PAUSE

On a diagonal to your left is the southeast corner of this intersection. PAUSE On this corner is an automobile tune-up center specializing in foreign cars. The front and side parking lots are usually filled with parked cars. The parking lot can be accessed from both streets. PAUSE

On a diagonal to your right is the southwest corner of this intersection. PAUSE On this corner is a shoppette. In the shoppette facing Alameda are a 7-11 convenience store, a financial service, a tax service, a tailor shop, a travel agency, and a beauty salon. One business, a dry cleaners, faces Garrison. The blacktop parking lot can be accessed from both streets. PAUSE

There is a pole on all four corners of the intersection. A cable is strung between these poles; a traffic light is suspended from each cable over the center of the street. One light faces each of the four directions. PAUSE

Now turn ninety degrees to your right to face westward on Alameda, a four-lane blacktop city street. PAUSE Now turn right ninety degrees again to once again face north on Garrison. PAUSE When I snap my fingers, you will return to your chair in your workshop. SNAP. PAUSE You may now awaken and open your eyes using the method you have learned.

For the second part of this exercise you will direct yourself in a manner similar to that used in the first part of the exercise. This time you will direct your awareness to the intersection of Kipling Street and Alameda Avenue in Lakewood, Colorado. This time speak out loud and record your impressions of what you see, sense, feel, and hear. After you have finished and open your eyes, do your writing exercise and then listen to your recorded psychic impressions. I have written what is at the intersection of Kipling and Alameda in the **Comments** section of this session so you can compare.

Now turn your recorder to RECORD, go to your workshop and then to Kipling and Alameda in Lakewood, Colorado, and verbally record everything you find there.

After Programming: Take your pen/pencil and paper and write the following—Session #12 is completed. Write the date. Sign your name. Be sure to use the writing modifications described earlier in this chapter. Then keep your paper as your record of achievement so you do not inadvertently skip a session.

Optional Additional Programming: This is an optional extra to help you tune yourself up even more. Do not substitute this exercise for the main programming cycle listed above. This is just an additional exercise if you want to hone yourself even more. You don't have to perform this optional exercise, but I recommend that you do if you have the extra time available to you. You can gain much if you do perform it, but you won't lose anything if you don't.

Go to your psychic workshop and do some more memory work similar to that in the Session #11 optional exercise.

Comments: Here is what is at the intersection of Kipling and Alameda in Lakewood, Colorado.

Kipling is a four-lane, divided blacktop city street that runs in a north-south direction.

Alameda is a four-lane, nondivided blacktop city street that runs in an east-west direction.

There is one traffic light pole on each corner that has a steel extension arm which holds the traffic light out over the center of the street.

The northwest corner is federal property and is bordered by a six-foot, barbed top, steel mesh fence. The corner itself has many trees and bushes and about a half-mile square of grass. About a half-mile back you can see the beginning of a large complex of various sized and shaped buildings that make up the Federal Center.

The northeast corner is undeveloped. There are some trees and many bushes. About a hundred yards back is a public mental health center which can be accessed only from Kipling. The mental health center is a red brick building.

The terrain drops sharply from the roadway on the southeast corner and there is a six-foot fence around the corner. At the bottom of the drop are trees and bushes. There are many trees on this corner. About a hundred yards from the corner, on Kipling, is a red brick church.

There is a small business complex built on a diagonal on the southwest corner so that the buildings half face each street. There is a blacktop parking lot that can be accessed only from Alameda. The businesses in this complex are: beauty shop, insurance office, bicycle shop, locksmith shop, swimming pool & spa business, and an alteration shop.

This is what the intersection looked like at the time this book was written. If you should sense something different, like a different business than the ones I have listed, you could very well be right because things might have changed since the book was written. However, I chose these two locations because they have been stable for many years, and the likelihood of major change is remote.

Session #13

Purpose: In this session you will take a quick world tour to ten places via your psychic projection. This conditions your mind to quickly (instantly) project from place to place and see, feel, sense, and hear information. It also establishes more reference points in your psychic center for future use.

Preparation: Get your tape recorder, a blank tape, paper and pen or pencil, a comfortable chair, and as quiet a location as you can. Take the phone off the hook.

Record the session written in italics in the **Programming Cycle** section by reading the words out loud and recording them on a cassette tape. Where instructions say PAUSE, stop talking for about three seconds or so while the tape continues to run. Then resume reading the italicized words. For longer pauses, the instructions will say STOP TALKING FOR X SECONDS while letting the tape continue to run. You can either use a watch or just count slowly (silently) to approximate the number of seconds. In place of X, the instructions will specify a number such as 10.

Programming Cycle: After you have recorded the following instructions (only record the italicized words), rewind the tape. Then relax in your chair, turn your recorder to PLAY, close your eyes and listen to the tape and follow the instructions given on the tape.

Go to your psychic workshop. STOP TALKING FOR 25 SECONDS. *Now take a deep breath and relax.* PAUSE *In a few moments you will begin a world tour, visiting ten different places. I will signal the change from one place to another by snapping my fingers. In each place you will have one minute to see, sense, feel, and hear what is there . . . to soak up the atmosphere and information in the place.*

It will be a different time of day in each of the places. Some may have daylight, some may have darkness. Some may be inhabited by people or creatures, others may not. Colors will vary. Each place is unique. Pay attention to everything—temperature, color, size, shape, sounds, the feel of the area, any signs of life and movement. PAUSE

Now it is time for your tour to begin. When I snap my fingers, you are to go to the north rim of the Grand Canyon in Arizona. SNAP. PAUSE *Investigate the Grand Canyon thoroughly.* STOP TALKING FOR 60 SECONDS.

When I snap my fingers, you are to go to Washington's Monument in Washington, D.C. SNAP. PAUSE *Investigate Washington's Monument thoroughly.* STOP TALKING FOR 60 SECONDS.

When I snap my fingers, you are to go to the Canadian side of Niagara Falls. SNAP. PAUSE *Investigate Niagara Falls thoroughly.* STOP TALKING FOR 60 SECONDS.

When I snap my fingers, you are to go to Victoria Falls in Africa. SNAP. PAUSE *Investigate Victoria Falls thoroughly. How does it compare to Niagara Falls?* STOP TALKING FOR 60 SECONDS.

When I snap my fingers, you are to go to the Eiffel Tower in Paris, France. SNAP. PAUSE *Investigate the Eiffel Tower thoroughly.* STOP TALKING FOR 60 SECONDS.

When I snap my fingers, you are to go to the Sahara Desert in North Africa. SNAP. PAUSE *Investigate the Sahara Desert thoroughly.* STOP TALKING FOR 60 SECONDS.

When I snap my fingers, you are to go to the North Pole of the Earth. SNAP. PAUSE *Investigate the North Pole thoroughly. How does the North Pole compare to the Sahara Desert?* STOP TALKING FOR 60 SECONDS.

When I snap my fingers, you are to go to the South Pole of the Earth. SNAP. PAUSE Investigate the South Pole thoroughly. How does the South Pole compare to the North Pole? STOP TALKING FOR 60 SECONDS.

When I snap my fingers, you are to go to the Great Wall of China. SNAP. PAUSE Investigate the Great Wall thoroughly. STOP TALKING FOR 60 SECONDS.

When I snap my fingers, you are to go to the Great Pyramid in Egypt. SNAP. PAUSE Investigate the Great Pyramid thoroughly. STOP TALKING FOR 60 SECONDS.

Now return to the Great Wall of China. SNAP. PAUSE Now back to the South Pole. SNAP. PAUSE Back to the North Pole. SNAP. PAUSE Back to the Sahara Desert. SNAP. PAUSE Back to the Eiffel Tower. SNAP. PAUSE Back to Victoria Falls. SNAP. PAUSE Back to Niagara Falls. SNAP. PAUSE Back to Washington's Monument. SNAP. PAUSE Back to the Grand Canyon. SNAP. PAUSE Back to your psychic workshop. SNAP. PAUSE Using the method you have learned, exit your workshop and open your eyes.

After Programming: Take your pen/pencil and paper and write the following—Session #13 is completed. Write the date. Sign your name. Be sure to use the writing modifications described earlier in this chapter. Then keep your paper as your record of achievement so you do not inadvertently skip a session.

Optional Additional Programming: This is an optional extra to help you tune yourself up even more. Do not substitute this exercise for the main programming cycle listed above. This is just an additional exercise if you want to hone yourself even more. You don't have to perform this optional exercise, but I recommend that you do if you have the extra time available to you. You can gain much if you do perform it, but you won't lose anything if you don't.

Wait approximately 6 to 12 hours after performing your main programming cycle, and repeat the main programming cycle. This will allow you to visit each place at a different time of day. Note any differences from the first visit.

Comments: This exercise is another building block in expanding your psychic experience and training your mind to respond to your will.

Session #14

Purpose: In this session you will take a quick tour of our universe, which is the Milky Way Galaxy, via your psychic projection. This conditions your mind to instantly project from place to place and see, sense, feel, and hear information. It also establishes more reference points in your psychic center for future use. You are learning to explore more and more things that are unknown to you. In the beginning, you explored what was familiar, and gradually you progressed toward that which is unfamiliar or even unknown to anyone.

Preparation: Get your tape recorder, a blank tape, paper and pen or pencil, a comfortable chair, and as quiet a location as you can. Take the phone off the hook.

Record the session written in italics in the **Programming Cycle** section by reading the words out loud and recording them on a cassette tape. Where instructions say PAUSE, stop talking for about three seconds or so while the tape continues to run. Then resume reading the italicized words. For longer pauses, the instructions will say STOP TALKING FOR X SECONDS while letting the tape continue to run. You can either use a watch or just count slowly (silently) to approximate the number of seconds. In place of

X, the instructions will specify a number such as 10.

Programming Cycle: After you have recorded the following instructions (only record the italicized words), rewind the tape. Then relax in your chair, turn your recorder to PLAY, close your eyes and listen to the tape and follow the instructions given on the tape.

Go to your psychic workshop. STOP TALKING FOR 25 SECONDS. *Now take a deep breath and relax.* PAUSE *In a few moments you will begin a tour of our universe, the Milky Way Galaxy. I will signal the change from one place to another by snapping my fingers.*

In each place you will have one minute to see, sense, feel, and hear what is there. Soak up the atmosphere and information in the place. Colors will vary. Each place is unique. Pay attention to everything. Temperature, color, size, shapes, sounds, terrain, atmosphere, the feel of the area, any signs of life and movement. PAUSE

Now it is time for your tour to begin. When I snap my fingers, you are to go to the Earth's Moon. SNAP. PAUSE *Investigate the Moon thoroughly.* STOP TALKING FOR 60 SECONDS.

When I snap my fingers, you are to go to our Sun. SNAP. PAUSE *Investigate the Sun thoroughly.* STOP TALKING FOR 60 SECONDS.

When I snap my fingers, you are to go to the planet Mercury. SNAP. PAUSE *Investigate Mercury thoroughly.* STOP TALKING FOR 60 SECONDS.

When I snap my fingers, you are to go to the planet Venus. SNAP. PAUSE *Investigate Venus thoroughly. How does it compare to Mercury?* STOP TALKING FOR 60 SECONDS.

When I snap my fingers, you are to go to the planet Mars. SNAP. PAUSE *Investigate Mars thoroughly.* STOP TALKING FOR 60 SECONDS.

When I snap my fingers, you are to go to the planet Jupiter.

SNAP. PAUSE *Investigate Jupiter thoroughly.* STOP TALKING FOR 60 SECONDS.

When I snap my fingers, you are to go to the planet Saturn. SNAP. PAUSE *Investigate Saturn thoroughly. How does Saturn compare to Jupiter?* STOP TALKING FOR 60 SECONDS.

When I snap my fingers, you are to go to the planet Uranus. SNAP. PAUSE *Investigate Uranus thoroughly. How does Uranus compare to Saturn?* STOP TALKING FOR 60 SECONDS.

When I snap my fingers, you are to go to the planet Neptune. SNAP. PAUSE *Investigate Neptune thoroughly.* STOP TALKING FOR 60 SECONDS..

When I snap my fingers, you are to go to the planet Pluto. SNAP. PAUSE *Investigate Pluto thoroughly.* STOP TALKING FOR 60 SECONDS.

When I snap my fingers, you are to go to the outer edge of the Milky Way Galaxy. SNAP. PAUSE *What is it like out here? Can you see beyond the Milky Way? What do you feel? Investigate the outer edge of the Milky Way thoroughly.* STOP TALKING FOR 60 SECONDS.

Now return to Pluto. SNAP. PAUSE *Now back to Neptune. SNAP.* PAUSE *Back to Uranus. SNAP.* PAUSE *Back to Saturn. SNAP.* PAUSE *Back to Jupiter. SNAP.* PAUSE *Back to Mars. SNAP.* PAUSE *Back to Venus. SNAP.* PAUSE *Back to Mercury. SNAP.* PAUSE *Back to the Sun. SNAP.* PAUSE *Back to the Moon. SNAP.* PAUSE *Now back to your psychic workshop. SNAP.* PAUSE

Using the method you have learned, exit your workshop and open your eyes.

After Programming: Take your pen/pencil and paper and write the following—Session #14 is completed. Write the date. Sign your name. Be sure to use the writing modifications described earlier in this chapter. Then keep your paper as your record of achievement so you do not inadvertently skip a session.

Optional Additional Programming: This is an optional extra to help you tune yourself up even more. Do not substitute this exercise for the main programming cycle listed above. This is just an additional exercise if you want to hone yourself even more. You don't have to perform this optional exercise, but I recommend that you do if you have the extra time available to you. You can gain much if you do perform it, but you will not lose anything if you don't.

Go back into the Milky Way Galaxy and examine black holes, stars, meteorites, asteroids, and whatever else you find.

Comments: This exercise is another building block in expanding your psychic awareness and experience. In the next session you will go beyond our galaxy to other universes.

Session #15

Purpose: In this session you explore the completely unknown. You will explore universes beyond ours. Science knows there are a great number of other universes, other galaxies, but that is about all that is known. Allow your intelligence to visit some other universes and record what your experience is.

Preparation: Get your tape recorder, a blank tape, paper and pen or pencil, a comfortable chair, and as quiet a location as you can. Take the phone off the hook.

You will use your recorder just to record what you experience during this session.

Programming Cycle: In this session you are on your own. Put your recorder on RECORD and then go to your psychic workshop. From your workshop, project to the outer edge of the Milky Way. Then project to another universe. Once you enter another universe, talk out loud to record your experiences, thoughts, feelings, and so forth. Visit as many other universes as you wish, making verbal records for each experience. When you finish, return to your psychic workshop and to the beta level of consciousness.

After Programming: Take your pen/pencil and paper and write the following—Session #15 is completed. Write the date. Sign your name. Be sure to use the writing modifications described earlier in this chapter. Then keep your paper as your record of achievement so you do not inadvertently skip a session.

Optional Additional Programming: Your choice. Do whatever you wish from the exercises you have already had up until now.

Comments: You now know from personal experience that you have the psychic ability to investigate any dimension you want to. You can go where no person has ever been before insofar as is known. Before this 30-session training period is over, you will also have experiences with deceased persons. The nonphysical part of your being is just as readily available to you as is the physical part of your being.

Session #16

Purpose: In this session you will project into another person's body. You will do this many more times before the end of this 30-session training period. This will be very similar to the session #10 exercise when you investigated your own body. Many people have apprehension about invading another person's space. First of all, you cannot harm them. You have been conditioned that your power will be lost if you try to harm someone. Remember your shield; it protects others from you as well as protecting you from the negativism of others.

Secondly, you are going to project to them so you can offer your help if they need it. It is true that you may become quite aware of their thoughts, secrets, fears, and so forth. That is why I have used the word "integrity" so many times in this book. What you discover psychically must remain your knowledge only; you do not have the right to gossip about what you discover. The gossip will only bring negative karma to you.

For this exercise, select a person whom you personally know fairly well. If you know someone who has health problems, select that person so you can offer your help psychically and also learn much psychically about abnormalities.

Preparation: Get your tape recorder, a blank tape, paper and pen or pencil, a comfortable chair, and as quiet a location as you can. Take the phone off the hook.

Record the session written in italics in the **Programming Cycle** section by reading the words out loud and recording them on a cassette tape. Where instructions say PAUSE, stop talking for about three seconds or so while the tape continues to run. Then resume reading the italicized words. For longer pauses, the instructions will say STOP TALKING FOR X SECONDS while letting the tape continue to run. You can either use a watch or just count slowly (silently) to approximate the number of seconds. In place of X, the instructions will specify a number such as 10.

Be sure to have a specific person in mind, someone you know personally, to invite into your psychic workshop for your psychic investigation.

Programming Cycle: After you have recorded the following instructions (only record the italicized words),
rewind the tape. Then relax in your chair, turn your recorder to PLAY, close your eyes and listen to the tape and follow
the instructions given on the tape.

Go to your psychic workshop. STOP TALKING FOR 25
SECONDS. *Now take a deep breath and relax.* PAUSE *Now
press your control button to open the door at the end of the
workshop and call out the name of the person whom you wish to
have enter your workshop.* PAUSE *Invite the person to enter.*
STOP TALKING FOR 6 SECONDS. *Greet your guest who has
just entered your workshop.* PAUSE

*When I snap my fingers, begin scanning your guest's exterior
from head to toe, front and back. Ask your guest to turn and walk
whenever you wish. Observe everything about the exterior of your
guest. Skin tone, scars, general appearance, everything. If you
detect any abnormality, correct it. You have two minutes. SNAP.*
STOP TALKING FOR 120 SECONDS.

*Now when I snap my fingers, physically reach out and lift
your guest's head off and place it over your own head. SNAP.*
PAUSE *You are now able to sense your guest's emotions, thought
patterns, fears, anxieties, personality, character and so forth. Ask
questions from your mind to your guest's mind. Before you finish,
send thoughts of love and well-being to your guest. You have two
minutes to investigate thoroughly.* STOP TALKING FOR
120 SECONDS.

*When I snap my fingers, physically reach up and remove
your guest's head from yours and put it back onto your guest's
body. SNAP.* STOP TALKING FOR 6 SECONDS.

*When I snap my fingers, project your intelligence into your
guest's head. SNAP.* PAUSE *You can now examine the head from
a physical standpoint. Be thorough. Examine everything in the
head. If you detect any abnormality, correct it. You have two
minutes.* STOP TALKING FOR 120 SECONDS.

When I snap my fingers, project your intelligence into your guest's skeleton in the skull. SNAP. PAUSE Now scan the entire skeletal system from head to toe thoroughly. If you detect any abnormality, correct it. You have two minutes. STOP TALKING FOR 120 SECONDS.

When I snap my fingers, project your intelligence into your guest's bloodstream. SNAP. PAUSE Allow yourself to be circulated completely through the bloodstream. Notice everything . . . cell structure, general appearance of health, color. If you detect any abnormality, correct it. You have two minutes. STOP TALKING FOR 120 SECONDS.

When I snap my fingers, project into your guest's chest cavity and lower body trunk and investigate all the organs there . . . the heart, the lungs, kidneys, bladder, stomach, liver, pancreas, sex organs, digestive system. If you detect any abnormality, correct it. You have four minutes. STOP TALKING FOR 240 SECONDS.

When I snap my fingers, begin scanning the parts of the body that you have not yet investigated . . . the hips, legs, feet, arms, hands, and anything else you wish to examine. If you detect any abnormality, correct it. You have two minutes. STOP TALKING FOR 120 SECONDS.

When I snap, go back to the chest cavity. SNAP. Back to the bloodstream. SNAP. Back to the skeleton. SNAP. Back to the head. SNAP. Back outside the body and into your chair. SNAP. PAUSE

Thank your guest for coming to visit. PAUSE Now say to your guest, "I love you and bless you and release you to your higher self." STOP TALKING FOR 10 SECONDS.

When I snap my fingers, your guest will leave your workshop through the door. SNAP. PAUSE Press your control button and close the door. Now you may leave your workshop and open your eyes when you are ready.

After Programming: Take your pen/pencil and paper and write the following—Session #16 is completed. Write

the date. Sign your name. Be sure to use the writing modifications described earlier in this chapter. Then keep your paper as your record of achievement so you do not inadvertently skip a session.

Optional Additional Programming: This is an optional extra to help you tune yourself up even more. Do not substitute this exercise for the main programming cycle listed above. This is just an additional exercise if you want to hone yourself even more. You don't have to perform this optional exercise, but I recommend that you do if you have the extra time available to you. You can gain much if you do perform it, but you will not lose anything if you don't.

Go to your workshop and repeat the main programming cycle, but with a different person whom you know personally.

Comments: After this exercise you probably are starting to feel like a real practicing psychic. You should feel this way because everything up to now has been to prepare you for exploring the unknown and especially for giving help to others who need it. That is what being a practicing psychic is all about.

Session #17

Purpose: This session is a departure from the kind of thing you have been doing. In this session you will experience communication with a deceased person. Deceased persons can be a source of valuable information for you. On a personal basis, you may want to know how someone you love is "over there." Or you may have questions about the death process itself. Or perhaps questions about life on the "other side." Sometimes deceased persons can bring you knowledge and information that you would not be able to obtain through any other source.

This may well be an emotional experience for you so be prepared for it. You will visit with a deceased person of your choice whom you knew very well in this life. Perhaps a parent, grandparent, child, spouse, close friend. If you start crying, that is all right. Just go ahead and cry, but do please remain in your workshop while you do it so you will not break the rapport you have with the person you are communicating with.

Just converse with your friend the same as you did when they were alive in body in the Earth plane. You will find that you can converse quite well mentally, but if you wish to talk out loud that is OK also.

Preparation: Get your tape recorder, a blank tape, paper and pen or pencil, a comfortable chair, and as quiet a location as you can. Take the phone off the hook.

Record the session written in italics in the **Programming Cycle** section by reading the words out loud and recording them on a cassette tape. Where instructions say PAUSE, stop talking for about three seconds or so while the tape continues to run. Then resume reading the italicized words. For longer pauses, the instructions will say STOP TALKING FOR X SECONDS while letting the tape continue to run. You can either use a watch or just count slowly (silently) to approximate the number of seconds. In place of X, the instructions will specify a number such as 10.

Have a specific deceased person in mind, whom you knew well, to invite into your psychic workshop.

Programming Cycle: After you have recorded the following instructions (only record the italicized words), rewind the tape. Then relax in your chair, turn your recorder to PLAY, close your eyes and listen to the tape and follow the instructions given on the tape.

Go to your psychic workshop. STOP TALKING FOR 25 SECONDS. *Take a deep breath and relax.* PAUSE *In order to get yourself completely calm and relaxed for your meeting with your deceased friend, count backwards with me from 10 to 1, allowing your breathing to become deeper and easier as you count. Ten, deeper, nine, eight, deeper and deeper, seven, six, feel yourself going deeper still, five, four, more and more relaxed, three, two, one.* PAUSE *Now press your control button to open the door.* PAUSE *Call out your friend's name mentally and invite him/her to enter your workshop for a visit.* STOP TALKING FOR 6 SEC-ONDS.

As your friend enters, I will talk no more. Stay and visit for as long as you wish and return to beta and awaken when you are finished. Before you leave be sure to tell your friend that you love them and that you bless them and release them to their higher self.

After Programming: Take your pen/pencil and paper and write the following—Session #17 is completed. Write the date. Sign your name. Be sure to use the writing modifications described earlier in this chapter. Then keep your paper as your record of achievement so you do not inadvertently skip a session.

Optional Additional Programming: This is an optional extra to help you tune yourself up even more. Do not substitute this exercise for the main programming cycle listed above. This is just an additional exercise if you want to hone yourself even more. You don't have to perform this optional exercise, but I recommend that you do if you have the extra time available to you. You can gain much if you do perform it, but you will not lose anything if you don't.

Select another deceased friend and visit with him/her in your workshop just as you did in the main programming cycle.

Comments: The experience you had in this session speaks for itself. You have opened up a vista to your psychic center that you didn't know you had. Use it as often as you wish. Get in the habit of blessing those, both living and deceased, that you work or visit with and releasing them to their higher self.

Session #18

Purpose: In this session you will once again visit with a deceased person. This time it will be with someone you do not know personally. You choose who the person will be. You may have a hero who is deceased. Or perhaps some famous deceased personality that you would like to talk to. Or maybe there was someone on the fringes of your own life whom you never had the opportunity to really know. Now is your chance to communicate with that person.

You will be on your own for this session. No tape recording to guide you. You should do nicely because you have plenty of experience now in bringing people and things into and out of your workshop. You know how to conduct yourself into and out of your psychic workshop. You know how to communicate, question, sense, feel, see, and hear at the psychic level.

Select the deceased person you wish to communicate with, and then go to your workshop and do it.

Preparation: Get paper and pen or pencil, a comfortable chair, and as quiet a location as you can. Take the phone off the hook.

Programming Cycle: Go to your psychic workshop and invite in the deceased person, whom you do not know personally, and communicate for as long as you wish.

After Programming: Take your pen/pencil and paper and write the following—Session #18 is completed. Write the date. Sign your name. Be sure to use the writing modifications described earlier in this chapter. Then keep your paper as your record of achievement so you do not inadvertently skip a session.

Optional Additional Programming: This is an optional extra to help you tune yourself up even more. Do not substitute this exercise for the main programming cycle listed above. This is just an additional exercise if you want to hone yourself even more. You don't have to perform this optional exercise, but I recommend that you do if you have the extra time available to you. You can gain much if you do perform it, but you will not lose anything if you don't.

Repeat the main programming cycle, but with a different deceased person whom you do not know personally.

Comments: By now, you are probably getting "high" on going to your workshop and investigating all the marvelous avenues of information available to you there. In retrospect, you probably think you had a dull life before going *Beyond Hypnosis*.

My friend, you are just beginning. Your real, profound, enlightening experiences will come *after* you finish this 30-session training period and continue to practice as a psychic every day.

Session #19

Purpose: In this session you will bring a person into your psychic workshop who is currently living in this Earth plane and whom you know personally. This will be a chance to visit with this person at the level of their higher mind, and yours. Perhaps there is a special person you have deep feelings for but have been unable, for lack of opportunity or courage, to speak frankly to. Now is the time you can express yourself. If you want to say, "I love you," do it.

Maybe there is a person you have been unable to get along with for one reason or another. Now is a chance to talk to that person openly, to say what is on your mind, to chew them out if that is what is appropriate, or to find out what is "bugging" them. Let them know you really want to be on good terms with them, and ask them to at least meet you halfway.

Maybe there is someone you suspect is having problems but you don't know what they are. Talk to that person in your psychic workshop. Ask them what the problem is and let them know of your concern. Tell them you want to help. Project love to them.

Do you want a raise or promotion? Talk to your boss about it in your workshop. Point out why you deserve it, and what you have done for the company.

Would you like your husband or wife to be more loving, less nagging, or whatever? Discuss it in your psychic workshop.

Again, you will be on your own with no tape recorder to guide you. Just select your person, go to your workshop, invite the person in and have your visit at the level of your higher mind. Stay as long as you wish. Remember, give the person your love, bless them, and release them to their higher self.

Preparation: Get paper and pen or pencil, a comfortable chair, and as quiet a location as you can. Take the phone off the hook.

Programming Cycle: Just go to your psychic workshop

and visit with the living person of your choice whom you know personally. Stay as long as you wish, returning to beta level using the method you have learned. Be sure to say, "I love you and bless you and release you to your higher self" before departing from your guest.

After Programming: Take your pen/pencil and paper and write the following—Session #19 is completed. Write the date. Sign your name. Be sure to use the writing modifications described earlier in this chapter. Then keep your paper as your record of achievement so you do not inadvertently skip a session.

Optional Additional Programming: This is an optional extra to help you tune yourself up even more. Do not substitute this exercise for the main programming cycle listed above. This is just an additional exercise if you want to hone yourself even more. You don't have to perform this optional exercise, but I recommend that you do if you have the extra time available to you. You can gain much if you do perform it, but you will not lose anything if you don't.

Repeat the main programming cycle but with a different person whom you know personally.

Comments: It is getting to be fun, isn't it? The payoff in this exercise comes when you watch the change in the interaction between you and the person whom you talked with during the exercise. The relationship will take a new turn, in a positive direction, and you will marvel at how truly effective your psychic ability is.

If you told someone you loved them, and you want them to notice you and become serious with you, watch out! Things may happen fast. Be sure you really wanted that person before you told them psychically, because there is a very good chance that you will succeed. I know of a case where a young man had a crush on a very pretty young lady who showed no interest in him whatsoever. He used his psychic abilities to court her. Sure enough, she began to warm up to him, and they finally married. To his chagrin, she turned out to be a habitual nag, and he had a miserable marriage.

So the word for the day is: Be careful of what you ask for, because you just might get it.

Session #20

Purpose: This session is similar to session #19. You will bring a living person into your psychic workshop and communicate with him/her. The person you select should be someone you do not know personally. This is your opportunity to visit with that person.

Perhaps there is a famous person you would love to meet and talk with. Do it!

Perhaps there is a publisher you would like to have accept your book for publication and offer you a contract. Do your negotiating in your psychic workshop at the level of your higher mind. Tell the publisher why your work should be accepted. Tell them what value your book has for their company. If your work is not professionally acceptable, be prepared for the publisher to tell you that in your workshop. Remember, this is a place to transmit and to receive valuable information. It is not a place for making undeserving wishes come true.

Again, you are on your own in this session with no tape recording to guide you. By now you know exactly what to do, so do it.

Preparation: Get your paper and pen or pencil, a comfortable chair, and as quiet a location as you can. Take the phone off the hook.

Programming Cycle: You know what to do, so do it!

After Programming: Take your pen/pencil and paper and write the following—Session #20 is completed. Write the date. Sign your name. Be sure to use the writing modifications described earlier in this chapter. Then keep your paper as your record of achievement so you do not inadvertently skip a session.

Optional Additional Programming: Bring other living people you do not know personally into your workshop and communicate with them at the level of your higher mind.

Comments: What a powerful tool your psychic level of mind is! See how you can use it for just about anything. Use it wisely and with integrity. Be sure to always depart from your guests with, "I love you and bless you and release you to your higher self."

Session #21

Purpose: In this session you will meet your two advisors. One is a male advisor; the other female. I have no idea who they are, nor do you. You won't know until you meet them in your psychic workshop.

Each of us, regardless of our gender, has both a male and a female nature. Each of us also has a male and a female advisor at the psychic level.

All intelligent creatures, both those in this Earthly plane and those deceased and in spirit, belong to the supreme cosmic intelligence. Any of these could be your advisors. They have always been with you, you just haven't been aware of them. Now you will finally meet them and start communicating with them whenever you wish.

You can consult with your advisors. For example, suppose you are trying to help some female who has problems. Or perhaps you are having difficulty getting along with some female. Go to your workshop and consult with your female advisor about the situation and how you can best handle it.

If the person is male, consult with your male advisor.

Suppose you have some serious career choices to make. Consult with your advisors. They can help you sort things out so you can make good choices.

Use your advisors freely. They are excellent channels of intelligence from the cosmic intelligence.

Preparation: Get your tape recorder, a blank tape, paper and pen or pencil, a comfortable chair, and as quiet a location as you can. Take the phone off the hook.

Record the session written in italics in the **Programming Cycle** section by reading the words out loud and recording them on a cassette tape. Where instructions say PAUSE, stop talking for about three seconds or so while the tape continues to run. Then resume reading the italicized words. For longer pauses, the instructions will say STOP TALKING FOR X SECONDS while letting the tape continue to run. You can either use a watch or just count slowly (silently) to approximate the number of seconds. In place of X, the instructions will specify a number such as 10.

Programming Cycle: After you have recorded the following instructions (only record the italicized words), rewind the tape. Then relax in your chair, turn your recorder to PLAY, close your eyes and listen to the tape and follow the instructions given on the tape.

Go to your psychic workshop. STOP TALKING FOR 25

SECONDS. *Take a deep breath and relax.* PAUSE *Press your control button to bring two chairs into your workshop for your advisors to sit on when they enter. Choose whatever kind of chairs you wish.* STOP TALKING FOR 10 SECONDS. *Place one chair on your right side, slightly in front of yours and at a ninety-degree angle so it faces you.* STOP TALKING FOR 6 SECONDS. *Place the other chair on your left side, slightly in front of yours at a ninety-degree angle so it faces you* STOP TALKING FOR 6 SECONDS. *Designate one chair for the male and the other for the female by putting an "M" for male on one chair and an "F" for female on the other chair. Which chair you designate for each is your choice.* STOP TALKING FOR 6 SECONDS.

Now press your control button to open the door into your workshop. PAUSE *Now mentally say, "I welcome my male advisor into my workshop. Please enter and sit in your chair."* STOP TALKING FOR 10 SECONDS. *Greet your male advisor. Ask his name. Study his appearance. Thank him for coming. Talk with him now for a few moments.* STOP TALKING FOR 30 SECONDS.

Now mentally say, "I welcome my female advisor into my workshop. Please enter and sit in your chair." STOP TALKING FOR 10 SECONDS. *Greet your female advisor. Ask her name. Study her appearance. Thank her for coming. Talk with her now for a few moments.* STOP TALKING FOR 30 SECONDS.

Your advisors will be here each time you enter your psychic workshop. PAUSE *Stay as long as you wish in your workshop now to get acquainted with your advisors and to consult with them. When you get ready to leave, tell them, "I love you, bless you, and release you to your higher self." Address each one separately by name for this departing statement.* PAUSE *Then exit your workshop in the usual manner when you are ready to leave.*

After Programming: Take your pen/pencil and paper and write the following—Session #21 is completed. Write the date. Sign your name. Be sure to use the writing modifications described earlier in this chapter. Then keep your paper as your record of achievement so you do not inadvertently skip a session.

Optional Additional Programming: Go back for another visit with your advisors if you wish.

Comments: You now have a powerful source of information and help through your two advisors.

You may find that they sometimes contact you in crucial moments even when you have not specifically gone to your workshop to consult with them. For instance, you may be about to make a decision to do something when one of your advisors bursts into your awareness with "No!" If that happens, heed it. At least put off the decision until you can go to your workshop and consult and obtain more detail.

Session #22

Purpose: Each person's existence comprises four domains: physical, mental, spiritual, and worldly. You have a Master for each of your four domains. Each Master is a superior intelligence who is with you at all times to help you if you need help. Usually (but not always) you must request help in order for it to be given. This is because you were given free will as an innate part of your creation, and the Masters will not interfere with your exercise of free will.

In this session you will get to meet your four Masters. The more you cultivate a good two-way rapport with them, the more enrichment will enter all phases of your life.

Preparation: Get your tape recorder, a blank tape, paper and pen or pencil, a comfortable chair, and as quiet a location as you can. Take the phone off the hook.

Record the session written in italics in the **Program-**

ming Cycle section by reading the words out loud and recording them on a cassette tape. Where instructions say PAUSE, stop talking for about three seconds or so while the tape continues to run. Then resume reading the italicized words. For longer pauses, the instructions will say STOP TALKING FOR X SECONDS while letting the tape continue to run. You can either use a watch or just count slowly (silently) to approximate the number of seconds. In place of X, the instructions will specify a number such as 10.

Programming Cycle: After you have recorded the following instructions (only record the italicized words), rewind the tape. Then relax in your chair, turn your recorder to PLAY, close your eyes and listen to the tape and follow the instructions given on the tape.

Enter your psychic workshop. STOP TALKING FOR 25 SECONDS. *Take a deep breath and relax.* PAUSE *At this moment your four Masters are not visible to you, but they are behind your chair. Shortly, you will be introduced to each one individually by invoking the Master's name with a request that the Master become known to you. The Master will then appear visibly in front of you. You should say, "Thank you for being here." Observe the Master's appearance. You will have time to spend a few moments with the Master before meeting the next Master.*

Each Master has the power to automatically alter your consciousness so you are in the same plane as the Master. This is what happens when you invoke the Master's name. That is why you can see the Master when you invoke the name. You do not have to be in your psychic workshop to invoke the presence of, and help from, a Master. You may be at beta when some sort of situation arises where you need the assistance of a Master. Just invoke the Master's help and presence. You will be automatically pulled into an altered state at the Master's level where help is available. PAUSE

Now it is time to meet your first Master. Mentally call out the

following words, "I ask my Master of Physical Matters to become known to me!" SNAP. PAUSE

Your Master of Physical Matters is now in front of you. Greet your Master. PAUSE *Observe the Master's appearance.* PAUSE *This Master has domain over your physical health and balance, your body functions, and your physical protection.* PAUSE *Spend a few moments now with your Master of Physical Matters.* STOP TALKING FOR 30 SECONDS.

Now it is time to meet your second Master. Mentally call out the following words, "I ask my Master of Mental Matters to become known to me!" SNAP. PAUSE

Your Master of Mental Matters is now in front of you. Greet your Master. PAUSE *Observe the Master's appearance.* PAUSE *This Master has domain over your mental health and balance, peace of mind, and your psychic functioning.* PAUSE *Spend a few moments now with your Master of Mental Matters.* STOP TALKING FOR 30 SECONDS.

Now it is time to meet your third Master. Mentally call out the following words, "I ask my Master of Spiritual Matters to become known to me!" SNAP. PAUSE

Your Master of Spiritual Matters is now in front of you. Greet your Master. PAUSE *Observe the Master's appearance.* PAUSE *This Master has domain over love, faith, truth, wisdom, courage, and integrity.* PAUSE *Spend a few moments now with your Master of Spiritual Matters.* STOP TALKING FOR 30 SECONDS.

Now it is time to meet your fourth Master. Mentally call out the following words, "I ask my Master of Worldly Matters to become known to me!" SNAP. PAUSE

Your Master of Worldly Matters is now in front of you. Greet your Master. PAUSE *Observe the Master's appearance.* PAUSE *This Master has domain over prosperity, success, and self-actualization.* PAUSE *Spend a few moments now with your master of Worldly Matters.* STOP TALKING FOR 30 SECONDS.

Thank all your Masters for being with you. PAUSE *Now take a deep breath and relax as your Masters leave your sight.*

PAUSE *Even when you do not see them, your Masters are always with you.* PAUSE
Now leave your workshop by your usual method.

After Programming: Take your pen/pencil and paper and write the following—Session #22 is completed. Write the date. Sign your name. Be sure to use the writing modifications described earlier in this chapter. Then keep your paper as your record of achievement so you do not inadvertently skip a session.

Optional Additional Programming: Go to your workshop and do whatever you wish.

Comments: If you need to communicate with one of your Masters, do so. You do not have to be in your psychic workshop. Just invoke the Master's name.

Do not play games just to see if a Master will respond. Your Masters are not obedient servants to appear and obey your whims. They are a superior intelligence available when you have a genuine need. Respect them and they will be a valuable strength for you in time of need.

If you attempt to "play games," you establish a "cry wolf" syndrome. Then when you really need assistance, it may not be available.

Session #23

Purpose: Once again you are to investigate a living person's mind and body, correct any abnormalities you may find, and make a recording as you go along.

It makes no difference whether it is someone you know personally or not. You might scan the newspaper for candidates. Usually the newspaper has the name of some person who is ill or has been injured. Sometimes you have a friend whose mother, brother, etc., is ill or injured. Try to collect at least four names and the city they are in (or live in) to use for this psychic work. You will just need one name for today's exercise, but you will need three more for session #27.

Do not overlook handicapped individuals, paraplegics, deaf or blind persons, etc. These people need all the help, love, courage, and peace you can send them. Investigating these people is also great training for you.

There are two reasons why so much emphasis is put on working with people's mental and physical condition. First, if you can do this successfully, you can do anything in the psychic realm; this is superb training for you. Second, it gives you the opportunity to start helping others with your energy; the entire thrust of being a practicing psychic is to enrich lives . . . others' and yours.

In this session you will use the recorder only to record your voice while you are performing in your psychic workshop. You are on your own to direct your own activity without the aid of recorded instructions.

Preparation: Get your tape recorder, a blank tape, paper and pen or pencil, a comfortable chair, and as quiet a location as you can. Take the phone off the hook.

Programming Cycle: Put your recorder on RECORD, then go to your psychic workshop and greet your advisors. Then work the case of the person you have selected just as you have learned from previous exercises. Consult with your advisors if you wish. Be sure to speak out loud and record what you are doing, what you see, feel, sense, and hear, and what corrective action (if any) you are taking. Be as specific as you can. Don't just say, "I am fixing a damaged liver." Tell exactly what it is about the liver that makes you believe it is damaged. Then tell exactly how you are fixing it.

Do not be concerned that you may sound foolish. You aren't foolish, and only you are going to know what is being said.

After Programming: Take your pen/pencil and paper and write the following—Session #23 is completed. Write the date. Sign your name. Be sure to use the writing modifications described earlier in this chapter. Then keep your paper as your record of achievement so you do not inadvertently skip a session.

Optional Additional Programming: Do what you wish as an optional extra.

Comments: By now, your psychic ability is becoming quite sensitive and effective. You are getting a good "feel" for what you are doing. You probably are also becoming quite confident in yourself. You will continue getting better and better the more you use your psychic ability, and this is so.

Session #24

Purpose: In this session you will return to the beach of time and the sea of cosmic consciousness. Once there, you will go forward in time to the year 2050 at the same geographical location where you are presently. You will have time there to explore and observe before returning to your psychic workshop.

Preparation: Get your tape recorder, a blank tape, paper and pen or pencil, a comfortable chair, and as quiet a location as you can. Take the phone off the hook.

Record the session written in italics in the **Programming Cycle** section by reading the words out loud and recording them on a cassette tape. Where instructions say

PAUSE, stop talking for about three seconds or so while the tape continues to run. Then resume reading the italicized words. For longer pauses, the instructions will say STOP TALKING FOR X SECONDS while letting the tape continue to run. You can either use a watch or just count slowly (silently) to approximate the number of seconds. In place of X, the instructions will specify a number such as 10.

Programming Cycle: After you have recorded the following instructions (only record the italicized words), rewind the tape. Then relax in your chair, turn your recorder to PLAY, close your eyes and listen to the tape and follow the instructions given on the tape.

Go to your psychic workshop and greet your advisors. STOP TALKING FOR 25 SECONDS. *Now take a deep breath and relax.* PAUSE *Press your control button to lower the entire wall at the end of your workshop into the floor to reveal the beach of time and the sea of cosmic consciousness beyond.* STOP TALKING FOR 10 SECONDS

Walk out onto the beach. PAUSE *Stop and stand for a moment facing the sea just where the dry sand meets the wet sand.* PAUSE *Notice the gulls circling above.* PAUSE *Listen to their squawks.* PAUSE *Look to your right. The sea and beach are endless. To your right is time past.* PAUSE *Look to your left. The sea and the beach are endless. To your left is time future.* PAUSE

As you continue looking to your left, a fog bank quickly moves in to obscure your vision in that direction. STOP TALKING FOR 10 SECONDS. *Now turn and walk to your left into the fog bank. Stop walking when you are completely surrounded by dense fog.* STOP TALKING FOR 10 SECONDS.

You are now moving forward in time very rapidly. PAUSE *Feel the damp fog swirling around you as you are transported forward in time.* PAUSE *Feel the energy changes.* PAUSE *Sense your movement.* PAUSE *In a moment, when I snap my fingers, the movement will stop, the fog will disappear, and you will find yourself in the year 2050 in the same geographical location as when you left your psychic workshop.* SNAP. PAUSE

The fog has disappeared. The year is 2050. Look around you. PAUSE *What is here? What is going on? Who or what is here? What do you see, feel, sense, and hear?* PAUSE *You will now have five minutes to explore the area, observing and remembering everything. When I next snap my fingers, the fog bank will return and surround you.* STOP TALKING FOR 5 MINUTES.

SNAP. *The fog bank has returned and it surrounds you.* PAUSE *You are now moving very rapidly back in time toward the time when you left your psychic workshop.* PAUSE *Feel the damp fog swirling around you as you are transported back in time.* PAUSE *Feel the energy changes.* PAUSE *Sense your movement.* PAUSE *When I snap my fingers, the movement will stop, the fog will disappear, and you will find yourself back on the beach of time in front of your workshop.* SNAP. PAUSE

The fog has disappeared. The time is the present. PAUSE *Walk back into your psychic workshop and sit in your chair.* PAUSE *Press your control button to raise the wall of your workshop back into its original position.* STOP TALKING FOR 10 SECONDS.

Stay in your workshop and reflect on your experience. Compare the year 2050 to the present. What changes, if any, took place? PAUSE *Consult with your advisors about your experience if you wish.* PAUSE *When you are ready to leave your workshop, thank your advisors for being there, tell them goodbye for now, and exit using your usual method.*

After Programming: Take your pen/pencil and paper and write the following—Session #24 is completed. Write the date. Sign your name. Be sure to use the writing modifications described earlier in this chapter. Then keep your paper as your record of achievement so you do not inadvertently skip a session.

Optional Additional Programming: Do more projections into the future at different times if you wish.

Comments: All time exists concurrently in different planes of awareness. It is only our earthly senses that perceive time as past, present, and future. That is why we are able to travel in time; we merely direct our awareness to the plane where that time already exists.

The plane of time past is stable. It does not change.

The plane of time present (where we perceive our current life) is constantly changing.

The plane of time future is also constantly changing because future always reflects the effects of time present (cause and effect action).

This brings up the question, "Can we then change the future by changing the present?" The answer is a resounding, "Yes!"

Here is a hypothetical case to illustrate this. Suppose you projected into the future and saw that next week a certain boat was going to run aground on an unknown shoal in its path. You immediately got in touch with the ship's Captain and alerted him to this unknown shoal. On his voyage, the Captain steered clear of the area and avoided the collision. You caused the future to change by taking an action in the present.

The reason you saw the collision in the first place is because all events that were currently in progress would eventually take the boat on a collision course. Once you entered the picture and alerted the boat's Captain, all the events changed, and thus the future changed. If you would have projected forward in time again after alerting the Captain, you would not have seen the collision even though the boat had not yet started its voyage. Of course, if the Captain had been predisposed to ignore your warning, you would still have seen the collision.

This is a difficult concept to grasp, I know. As you gain experience in psychic matters, you will gain a clearer understanding of these matters.

History is full of cases where a psychic gave a warning which was ignored, producing dire results. Julius Caesar was warned not to go to the Senate on the Ides of March. He went anyway and was murdered.

You would probably be well advised to not spend much time looking into the future. If you run around shouting all sorts of warnings, you will be regarded as a "crazy" and likely will lose credibility. If your warnings materialize, then you are apt to be blamed for causing the problem. Use much discretion, wisdom, and restraint in looking into the future.

The present is where your current learning experience is. Take care of today with integrity, and you will have no need to be anxious about tomorrow.

Session #25

Purpose: In this session you are going to repair the world. You will not have recorded instructions to guide you, nor will you need to record what you are doing. In the **Programming Cycle** section instructions I will give you some general ideas and instructions of what to do, but by and large it will be your imagination and ingenuity that will get the job done.

You will spend as much time at a psychic level as you need to in order to do all the repair work you want. If there is so much to do that the time is too short, exit your workshop and go back later in the day to finish. There is no optional exercise for this session because this one exercise is a big one in terms of your time.

Preparation: Get your paper and pen or pencil, a comfortable chair, and as quiet a location as you can. Take the phone off the hook.

Programming Cycle: Enter your workshop and greet your advisors. Tell them you are going to repair the world and ask them to help you. Then project into outer space where you can view the Earth. Then turn the Earth as you wish to bring whatever part of the world you want into your view.

Correct those things that need it, for example, wars, famine, drought, pollution, crime, needless slaughter of whales, seals, etc. (whatever you perceive as a problem).

You might have a huge, powerful vacuum cleaner to draw off all the polluted air. You might have a huge, powerful magnet that draws off all weapons of war from every country, which you can then dump into the Sun where they will be instantly destroyed. You can plant two olive trees with white doves in the branches (these are universal symbols of peace) in each country so the symbols can multiply and bring peace to that country. Use your imagination and ingenuity to deal with the problems.

Some areas of the Earth to pay particular attention to are: first, spend the most time putting your own country into balance. Then deal with any parts of the world where there is war. Be sure to deal with famine, hunger, sickness and drought where it is rampant. Erase the stratification of races and classes wherever that is a problem.

Your objective is to build a world of love, peace, and prosperity for all. Get rid of the negative and replace it with the positive.

A big job, to be sure! Your efforts in this session are an excellent beginning. It can be done!

After Programming: Take your pen/pencil and paper and write the following—Session #25 is completed. Write

the date. Sign your name. Be sure to use the writing modifications described earlier in this chapter. Then keep your paper as your record of achievement so you do not inadvertently skip a session.

Optional Additional Programming: None.

Comments: A journey of a thousand miles begins with the first step. In this session you took that first important step. Feel good about it!

Session #26

Purpose: In this session you will return to the beach of time and the sea of cosmic consciousness. Once there, you will go backward in time to the year 1850 at the same geographical location where you are presently. You will have time there to explore and observe before returning to your psychic workshop.

Preparation: Get your tape recorder, a blank tape, paper and pen or pencil, a comfortable chair, and as quiet a location as you can. Take the phone off the hook.

Record the session written in italics in the **Programming Cycle** section by reading the words out loud and recording them on a cassette tape. Where instructions say PAUSE, stop talking for about three seconds or so while the tape continues to run. Then resume reading the italicized words. For longer pauses, the instructions will say STOP TALKING FOR X SECONDS while letting the tape continue to run. You can either use a watch or just count slowly (silently) to approximate the number of seconds. In place of X, the instructions will specify a number such as 10.

Programming Cycle: After you have recorded the following instructions (only record the italicized words), rewind the tape. Then relax in your chair, turn your recorder to PLAY, close your eyes and listen to the tape and follow the instructions given on the tape.

Go to your psychic workshop and greet your advisors. STOP TALKING FOR 25 SECONDS. *Now take a deep breath and relax.* PAUSE *Press your control button to lower the entire wall at the end of your workshop into the floor to reveal the beach of time and the sea of cosmic consciousness beyond.* STOP TALKING FOR 10 SECONDS.

Walk out onto the beach. PAUSE *Stop and stand for a moment facing the sea just where the dry sand meets the wet sand.* PAUSE *Notice the gulls circling above.* PAUSE *Listen to their squawks.* PAUSE *Look to your left. The sea and beach are endless. To your left is time future.* PAUSE *Look to your right. The sea and the beach are endless. To your right is time past.* PAUSE

As you continue looking to your right, a fog bank quickly moves in to obscure your vision in that direction. STOP TALKING FOR 10 SECONDS. *Now turn and walk to your right into the fog bank. Stop when you are completely surrounded by dense fog.* STOP TALKING FOR 10 SECONDS.

You are now moving backward in time very rapidly. PAUSE *Feel the damp fog swirling around you as you are transported backward in time.* PAUSE *Feel the energy changes.* PAUSE *Sense your movement.* PAUSE

In a moment, when I snap my fingers, the movement will stop, the fog will disappear, and you will find yourself in the year 1850 in the same geographical location as when you left your psychic workshop. SNAP. PAUSE

The fog has disappeared. The year is 1850. Look around you. PAUSE *What is here? What is going on? Who or what is here? What do you see, feel, sense, and hear?* PAUSE *You will now have five minutes to explore the area, observing and remembering everything. When I next snap my fingers, the fog bank will return and surround you.* STOP TALKING FOR 5 MINUTES.

SNAP. The fog bank has returned and it surrounds you. PAUSE *You are now moving very rapidly forward in time toward the time when you left your psychic workshop.* PAUSE *Feel the damp fog swirling around you as you are transported forward in time.* PAUSE *Feel the energy changes.* PAUSE *Sense your movement.* PAUSE *When I snap my fingers, the movement will stop, the fog will disappear, and you will find yourself back on the beach of time in front of your workshop. SNAP.* PAUSE

The fog has disappeared. The time is the present. PAUSE *Walk back into your psychic workshop and sit in your chair.* PAUSE *Press your control button to raise the wall of your workshop back into its original position.* STOP TALKING FOR 10 SECONDS.

Stay in your workshop and reflect on your experience. Compare the year 1850 to the present. What changes, if any, have taken place? PAUSE *Consult with your advisors about your experience if you wish.* PAUSE

When you are ready to leave your workshop, thank your advisors for being there, tell them goodbye for now, and exit using your usual method.

After Programming: Take your pen/pencil and paper and write the following—Session #26 is completed. Write the date. Sign your name. Be sure to use the writing modifications described earlier in this chapter. Then keep your paper as your record of achievement so you do not inadvertently skip a session.

Optional Additional Programming: Do more projections into the past at different times if you wish.

Comments: Exploring the past can be useful if you are searching for buried artifacts, lost civilizations, etc. It also can be useful for explaining some of the circumstances that exist in the present, or for learning how to avoid past mistakes.

Beyond these sorts of things, studying the past is like reading a stack of canceled checks. It is superficially interesting, but not especially valuable.

Again, I want to stress the present. Your life is NOW, not YESTERDAY, not TOMORROW. Just NOW. Live NOW. Learn NOW. Enjoy NOW. Do good NOW. Enrich your life NOW. In so doing, you automatically ensure a marvelous future and create what will become a great past.

To paraphrase the Persian poet Omar Khayyam, "Why fret about the unborn tomorrow? There is no tomorrow. Tomorrow has not come. Tomorrow may never come. There is only today, and today is ours."

Session #27

Purpose: In this session you will psychically investigate the mental and physical condition of three people of your choice, correct any abnormalities you may detect, and make a recording as you go along.

Preparation: Get your tape recorder, a blank tape, paper and pen or pencil, a comfortable chair, and as quiet a location as you can. Take the phone off the hook.

Programming Cycle: Put your recorder on RECORD, then go to your psychic workshop, greet your advisors, and then begin working the three cases you have selected, one at a time. Be sure to speak out loud and record what you are doing, what you see, feel, sense, and hear, and what specific corrective action (if any) you are taking. Consult with your advisors if you wish.

After Programming: Take your pen/pencil and paper

and write the following—Session #27 is completed. Write the date. Sign your name. Be sure to use the writing modifications described earlier in this chapter. Then keep your paper as your record of achievement so you do not inadvertently skip a session.

Optional Additional Programming: Work additional cases if you wish.

Comments: Today is a pregraduation exercise and is the culmination of all you have learned. Your performance today reflects the degree of expertness you have achieved due to your diligent efforts.

Session #28

Purpose: This exercise programs your mind for a shorter, faster method of entering into and exiting from your psychic workshop. You can use this method from now on.

Preparation: Get your tape recorder, a blank tape, paper and pen or pencil, a comfortable chair, and as quiet a location as you can. Take the phone off the hook.

Record the session written in italics in the **Programming Cycle** section by reading the words out loud and recording them on a cassette tape. Where instructions say PAUSE, stop talking for about three seconds or so while the tape continues to run. Then resume reading the italicized words. For longer pauses, the instructions will say STOP TALKING FOR X SECONDS while letting the tape continue to run. You can either use a watch or just count slowly (silently) to approximate the number of seconds. In place of X, the instructions will specify a number such as 10.

Programming Cycle: After you have recorded the

following instructions (only record the italicized words), rewind the tape. Then relax in your chair, turn your recorder to PLAY, close your eyes and listen to the tape and follow the instructions given on the tape.

Take a deep breath and mentally visualize and repeat the number 3 and see yourself quickly enter the ground floor of your skyscraper of consciousness. Once again, visualize and repeat the number 3 as you see yourself enter the UP elevator. Again, visualize and repeat the number 3 and see yourself arriving at the door marked DEEPEST ALPHA.

Now visualize and repeat the number 2 as you leave the elevator. Once again, visualize and repeat the number 2 as you quickly float down the hallway, passing over the squares with colored numbers 10 on down through 4. Again visualize and repeat the number 2 as you quickly descend the three steps to the door labeled TO THETA. Now mentally visualize and repeat the number 1 as you walk through the theta door. Once again, mentally visualize and repeat the number 1 as you rapidly sail down your staircase. Again visualize and repeat the number 1 as you swiftly move to your chair and sit down. PAUSE *Take a deep breath and relax.* PAUSE

In the future, you can enter theta and your psychic workshop by counting down and visualizing the numbers 3-2-1 while having a very rapid visualization or awareness of entering your skyscraper, going to the deepest alpha floor, moving to the theta door and through it, and down your staircase and into your chair. You will sense moving through the procedure at a high rate of speed, seeing things in a blur at times, yet with full awareness of what is happening. The 3-2-1 countdown with the accompanying visualization will take just a few seconds and you will be transported to your psychic workshop in the theta region, and this is so. PAUSE

To exit your workshop, all you will need to do is take a deep breath, and, as you exhale, mentally see yourself rapidly moving

up your psychic staircase, down the hall into the elevator, exiting the elevator on the ground floor and then open your eyes, wide awake and feeling fine. PAUSE *Try it now. Return to beta and open your eyes. I will give you 5 seconds this first time.* STOP TALKING FOR 5 SECONDS, TAPE STILL RUNNING.

Now close your eyes again and re-enter your workshop by the 3-2-1 countdown method you just learned. I will give you 10 seconds this first time. STOP TALKING FOR 10 SECONDS, TAPE RUNNING.

You are seated in your chair in your workshop once again. Now return to beta in 3 seconds. PAUSE *Very good. Now return to your workshop in 6 seconds.* STOP TALKING FOR 6 SECONDS, TAPE RUNNING. *Excellent. Your mind is responding well. Take a deep breath and relax.* PAUSE *From now on, the more you use the rapid entry and exit methods you have just learned, the faster you will become and the deeper you will go. With practice, you will soon enter your workshop instantly when you close your eyes, and you will return to beta instantly by just opening your eyes.* PAUSE *Now take a deep breath and awaken.*

After Programming: Take your pen/pencil and paper and write the following—Session #28 is completed. Write the date. Sign your name. Be sure to use the writing modifications described earlier in this chapter. Then keep your paper as your record of achievement so you do not inadvertently skip a session.

Optional Additional Programming: This is an optional extra to help you tune yourself up even more. Do not substitute this exercise for the main programming cycle listed above. This is just an additional exercise if you want to hone yourself even more. You don't have to perform this optional exercise, but I recommend that you do if you have the extra time available to you. You can gain much if you do perform it, but you will not lose anything if you don't.

Practice entering and exiting your workshop by your newly learned fast method. Do this periodically throughout the day. It just takes a few seconds and is superb mental training.

Comments: In everyday life you really need to go to your workshop instantly for many kinds of things. That is why it is important to train yourself to do so.

Here is a sampling of some uses where you need instantaneous responsiveness.

1. You are negotiating with a salesman for a purchase (say a new auto). You want to know if the salesman is being honest or deceitful. Instantly drop into your workshop and ask his higher mind via your higher mind, "Are you lying to me?" or whatever question you deem appropriate. You will get your answer, and then you will know what course you wish to follow. Total time lapse: probably one to three seconds.

2. You accidentally touch your finger against a hot burner on the stove. Drop instantly into your workshop and put psychic medication on it while saying something like: "No pain, perfect healing, no blister, no infection, no scar." Visualize a perfect, unharmed finger. Total time lapse: probably one to five seconds.

3. Someone asks you a question, and the answer seems to escape you (such as in test taking). Drop into your workshop. There you have a variety of choices. You can ask an advisor, or look up the answer in your library, or project the information on your psychic screen, or ask for an expert on the subject to enter your workshop and give you the information. Quite often you will just "know" the answer as soon as you enter your workshop. Total time lapse: probably one to ten or fifteen seconds, depending on what you do when in your workshop.

The more you use your workshop, the faster you get

responses and the more meaningful will your experiences become. If you are sloppy in your practice, expect sloppy results.

You should go to your workshop at least once every day. To become expert, at least three times every day. Once you have become expert, you will automatically spend most of your time there while conducting the affairs of your life. You will not need your eyes closed to enter your workshop or to remain there. When this time comes, you will know it. You will find you make fewer mistakes, make better choices, and are always happy.

How long does it take to become expert? It depends on your innate ability, your integrity, and your disciplined practice. In truth, you are not likely to reach absolute expertness or perfection in one lifetime; it is an eternal quest. You can, however, reach a very acceptable level of expertness where you can greatly enrich your life and the lives of others.

Session #29

Purpose: This session puts you completely on your own to perform as a psychic in any manner you choose. No suggestions or directions are given, no tape recorder. In day-to-day activities, you must function as a psychic on your own. This session gives you some practice.

Preparation: Get your paper and pen or pencil, a comfortable chair, and as quiet a location as you can. Take the phone off the hook. Just decide what you want to do in your workshop.

Programming Cycle: Go to your workshop and do whatever you wish. Awaken when you are finished.

After Programming: Take your pen/pencil and paper and write the following—Session #29 is completed. Write the date. Sign your name. Be sure to use the writing modifications described earlier in this chapter. Then keep your paper as your record of achievement so you do not inadvertently skip a session.

Optional Additional Programming: Just do more of the same.

Comments: In this session you put into practice all the things you have learned in a very real everyday way. You are now a practicing psychic. In the next session you will graduate in a special exercise.

Session #30

Purpose: This is your graduation session, and you will have a very special party in your workshop. This may be an emotional experience for you. It certainly will be a beneficial experience.

Preparation: Get your tape recorder, a blank tape, paper and pen or pencil, a comfortable chair, and as quiet a location as you can. Take the phone off the hook.

Record the session written in italics in the **Programming Cycle** section by reading the words out loud and recording them on a cassette tape. Where instructions say PAUSE, stop talking for about three seconds or so while the tape continues to run. Then resume reading the italicized words. For longer pauses, the instructions will say STOP TALKING FOR X SECONDS while letting the tape continue to run. You can either use a watch or just count slowly (silently) to approximate the number of seconds. In place of X, the instructions will specify a number such as 10.

Programming Cycle: After you have recorded the following instructions (only record the italicized words), rewind the tape. Then relax in your chair, turn your recorder to PLAY, close your eyes and listen to the tape and follow the instructions given on the tape.

Go to your psychic workshop. STOP TALKING FOR 6 SECONDS, TAPE RUNNING. *Take a deep breath and relax.* PAUSE *This is your graduation session. You have successfully completed your self-administered training to become a practicing psychic in order to enrich your life and the lives of others.* PAUSE

You are now going to have a special graduation party here in your psychic workshop. You can invite whomever you choose. Select those persons who have very special meaning to you. They may be persons who are living whom you know personally. They may be living persons whom you admire but do not know personally. They may be deceased persons you knew personally. They may be deceased persons whom you admired but did not know personally. The guest list is entirely your choice. You may invite a special pet, living or deceased, if you wish. It is your party. PAUSE

Your guests will enter one at a time from the door at the end of your workshop when you summon them. As each enters, he or she will take a place near you, forming a circle completely around you. Your chair will turn completely around so you will be able to easily see all of them. PAUSE

You should use this procedure to summon and greet your guests. Mentally call out, "I wish (say the guest's name) to enter my workshop." Watch that guest then enter through the door. Then say, "(Name of guest) I welcome you." The guest will automatically walk over and stand in the correct position. Repeat this procedure for each guest until a circle is formed around you with all the guests you wish to have at your graduation. I will give you two minutes to invite your guests. STOP TALKING FOR 120 SECONDS, TAPE RUNNING.

All your guests are in place now in a circle around you. All are facing you. PAUSE *Your guests have a collective gift for you. A gift of their deep love. All together now they begin radiating their love toward you in the center of the circle. The energy is so vibrant and intense that you can physically feel it. For the next 30 seconds just relax and absorb this tremendous gift of love. Feel it. Sense it. Absorb it.* STOP TALKING FOR 30 SECONDS, TAPE RUNNING.

Now it is your turn to give a gift of love to your guests. One at a time, look at each guest and say, "(Name of guest) I send you love." You have two minutes to do this. STOP TALKING FOR 120 SECONDS, TAPE RUNNING. *You have now given your gift to each guest.* PAUSE

Now it is time to receive your graduation blessing. Have the guests in front of you open up a path between you and the door at the end of the room. In a moment, I will ask you to push your control button. When you push it, the door will open and the Master of all Masters will enter and proceed directly to you. The Master of all Masters will encompass you and impress on your mind what your special ability is and what you are to do with your life. No one but you will know the message the Master of all Masters gives you. Now press your control button and allow the door to open. PAUSE

The Master of all Masters enters, bathed in the most brilliant light you have ever seen, and proceeds directly to you. You, too, are now bathed in the brilliant light. The Master of all Masters' energy impregnates your entire being, and the personal message is impressed onto your awareness. STOP TALKING FOR 10 SECONDS. *You now know who you are and what needs to be done that you can do. You have your personal charter.* STOP TALKING FOR 6 SECONDS, TAPE RUNNING. *Now the Master of all Masters is gone. Your guests are gone. But you are not alone because you have them all as part of you now . . . forever.* PAUSE

Stay in your workshop as long as you wish and reflect on the

message the Master of all Masters gave you. Awaken when you are ready.

After Programming: Take your pen/pencil and paper and write the following—Session #30 is completed. Write the date. Sign your name. Be sure to use the writing modifications described earlier in this chapter. Then keep your paper as your record of achievement.

Optional Additional Programming: No optional exercises today. You are now on your own.

Comments: After the experience you just had, my words would be inadequate. Just dwell on your own thoughts.

Summary

Just about everything has been said. Your own experience in completing this 30-session training speaks far more eloquently to you now than my words.

I will share one personal experience that spanned a number of years which might put some things into perspective for you.

In February 1972 I received my two advisors into my workshop. They were Ernest Hemingway and a nameless young woman. I did not request these advisors specifically; I just asked my two advisors to enter, and they are the ones I received. My workshop was circular and domed and was filled with a soft, orange glow. My chair was a leather recliner. I used this workshop daily for about two years or so. My advisors furnished me with much valuable help and advice.

Then one day I altered my consciousness to enter my workshop and something strange happened. Instead of entering my usual workshop, I began soaring over the Atlantic Ocean, then over Egypt. I landed inside the Great Pyramid in Egypt. I was sitting in a huge stone chair. Ramses II was on my right and an Egyptian woman on my left.

I asked, "What is this all about?"

"This is your new workshop, and we are your new advisors," Ramses II answered.

"Why?" I asked.

"Because you now need a different level of experience and knowledge," he answered.

For several more years, this was my new workshop. I went there daily and received knowledge and had experiences that I could not have even dreamed of before.

Then one day, when I tried to go to my workshop, something strange happened again. It was as though I was somewhere in space. The entire universe seemed clearly visible. There was a bright light that was pulling me toward it, and I entered the bright light.

"What is happening? Where am I? Where are my advisors?" were thoughts that raced through my mind.

Though I saw nothing or no one except the light, I was instantly impregnated with the answers to my questions. "You are in communication with the Source. Take counsel with self." I was given other awareness also, but that shall remain my private knowledge. Since then, I have gone within and taken counsel with self, which is the most direct line to the Source. I have had the most extraordinary experiences.

Will your experiences be similar to mine? I have no idea. We are each unique and have our own charters. You will experience what you need, exactly when you need it, and in the manner that is exactly right for you. That is all I can say with certainty. But be prepared for change, for the unexpected, and for the opening up of your awareness in ways you are not yet able to envision.

PASS IT ON

*What goes around
Must come around;
That is the law.
If you reap good
Then sow your good;
Just pass it on.*

*The law of ten
is for all men;
Spend some, get more
Horde not your love
Lest you stop love;
Just pass it on.*

CHAPTER 6

FOR GRADUATES

Those of you who have completed the psychic self-development sessions exactly as described in Chapter 5 are now graduate Practicing Involved Psychics, or **PIPs**, as I shall refer to you in this chapter. Practicing, because you are now committed to making your newly awakened psychic abilities a living part of your everyday activities. Involved, because you are involved in using your powerful mental powers to enrich your own life and the lives of all with whom you interact. Psychic, because you have now learned how to function at the natural psychic levels of your mind. It is appropriate that Practicing Involved Psychic forms the acronym PIP because the dictionary defines "pip" as: "something remarkable of its kind." And you graduates certainly are something remarkable of your kind. There will be a great deal more said shortly about PIPs and PIP activities.

Now what?

You have just completed a powerful basic training in the use of your mind as a practicing psychic. Where do you go from here?

Do you continue to study? Or, do you start using your training every day to achieve . . . to grow spiritually and to enrich your life and the lives of others? The answer to both questions is "Yes!"

Continued Study

Life, if lived to the fullest, is a constant quest for knowledge. So yes, continue to study, but with one proviso: study judiciously.

What does study judiciously mean?

In the introduction of this book I said there are many people who know the price of everything and the value of nothing. These are people like the ivory-tower professors we have all heard about who can quote every date, name, and event since the dawn of history, but are unable to perform the simple task of making reservations and purchasing tickets to visit the places they know so much about.

The pursuit of learning can be like that if you allow it. I know people who relentlessly pursue every course available that has anything to do with psychic phenomena, hypnosis, mind control, dreams, telepathy, etc. They can hardly wait for one course to end so they can start another. They read all the "in" books on the subjects. They have read about rolfing, rebirthing, out of body travel, all of Edgar Cayce's books, and on and on. These people are terrific conversationalists at parties. Yet with all this "learning" they are unable to get rid of a simple headache without taking two aspirin. Yet getting rid of a headache is perhaps the easiest of all mental exercises.

The irony is that the courses they took were all great, worthwhile courses. The books they read were all great, worthwhile books. Then why didn't they learn? Because learning is not a pursuit, it is a *process* that starts deep within self.

It is in the context of *process* that I will now discuss your further study.

At this moment, you have brought yourself into the realm of the psychic world. But, also at this moment, you don't realize or understand the full scope of what you have at your beck and call. You cannot possibly know until you begin to use, every day, your new-found psychic abilities. Therefore, your next logical learning experience should be: learn by doing.

For the time being, I recommend you put additional formal psychic study and classes on the back burner. There are various religions, cults, and organizations that have their own teachings for psychic development and use, and they are good courses of study. But for now, give yourself a fair chance to develop and use what you have gotten in this book before jumping into further study. I estimate that you should wait to do further formal study for at least one year. There are many roads to psychic development and practice. If you keep switching roads you end up doing a lot of traveling, but you may not reach your destination. Or at least, it may take you much longer to reach your destination.

In the meantime, do some casual reading to augment your daily psychic practice. The idea now is to allow yourself to experience and learn at the rate that is best for you. If you try to force too much too quickly you end up actually setting yourself back.

If I were to suggest a typical plan for you to follow, it might go something like this:

1. Start today, and continue every day from now on to use your psychic powers. Use everything you have learned in this book. This chapter contains many specific things you can begin with immediately. You will find others as you develop.

2. After about the first month of pure practicing as stated in item #1, select a book from the recommended list

in Appendix A and casually read it. Continue with your daily psychic practice, of course. Or select some book that is not in Appendix A if you wish. Since each of you is unique, the reading selection that is best for you is unique. As a generalization, a good starter book would be either *Hypnosis*, because it relates heavily to *Beyond Hypnosis*, or perhaps the booklet *As a Man Thinketh.*

3. After another month or so, select another book and read it casually. Of course, continue daily psychic practice. A good book about this time might be either *Psycho-Cybernetics* or *Wisdom of the Mystic Masters.*

4. Continue as in items #2 and #3 preceding. Books by Emmet Fox will have more meaning for you after you have become proficient as a practicing psychic. You may want to delay reading these books until after a year or more of psychic practice and experience.

5. After a year or so of self-development of your psychic powers, you can determine for yourself whether or not you want further formal training. You will probably have an awareness by this time concerning your future course of action. If not, ask your Masters. Probably ninety percent of you (my guess) will not want or need further formal study because you will have discovered how to learn and grow through your own developed faculties.

Some years ago my Masters told me to stop formal studying and to use what I already had. It was great advice, and I took it. I now learn through my own psychic faculties, which I occasionally augment with casual reading. My psychic faculties even lead me to what I need to read when I need to read it.

6. By following these first five steps you will ingrain psychic practice as your everyday way of life in every facet of your life. That is where you need to be.

Then you will begin to know the value, and not just the price, of everything.

Now read on for some specific suggestions that you, as a PIP, can immediately start implementing in order to reach your psychic development goals.

Try all of the things suggested in this chapter. Try any other things that may strike your fancy. That is the only way you can discover what you are best at and what interests you most. Once you discover your strengths, then concentrate on them to really start achieving all the enrichment you can.

You will find that there are some things that just don't work out for you at all, while other things work out very well. That is normal. Don't fret about what you are not able to do. Be glad for what you can do, and then do it.

For example, I have had zero success with out-of-body experience. My telepathic ability as a "sender" is above average, but as a "receiver" I am about average. I've had great successes (and a few nonsuccesses) in healing. I've had great successes in communicating with my Masters and Higher Mind. My Masters gave me the material for this book, for example. However, with psychometry I am perhaps only average. I have not done well at all on finding missing persons. And so on.

So it will be for you. Some things will be your expertise; others will not.

Psychic Living . . . A New Way of Life

PIPs fall into one of two general categories: joiners and loners. Both groups have essentially the same goal . . . to develop and use their innate psychic ability to the fullest possible extent for the enrichment of their life and the lives of others. The groups differ only in how they go about their psychic practice.

Joiners prefer to be part of a formal group and to participate with others along clearly defined lines. This usually means following certain rules that are determined by someone else or by a committee.

Loners prefer to work on their own at their own pace with no rules other than those they choose to make for themselves. I am a member of this group.

There is nothing wrong with either group. Whichever group suits you is the one to function in. Each group has advantages and disadvantages. To mention a couple:

Joiners

1. Group companionship and influence act as a pressure to make one continue psychic practice when one would rather not be so diligent. This means that if you don't have as much self-discipline as you want or need, the group will act as your discipline.

2. Group rules sometimes tend to restrict psychic development except along predefined paths. This means you may not get to do all the things you want to do when you want to do them or in the manner you think is best.

Loners

1. You must have great self-discipline because there is no one there to push you.

2. You are not bound by someone else's rules. You can do what you want when you want in the manner you want.

Networking

Both joiners and loners can gain through networking with others in practicing their psychic abilities. I *do* heartily recommend that you seriously consider working occasionally with other psychics.

As a PIP you can do all the things you want to do as an individual. In addition, you have the opportunity to team up from time to time with PIP pals to achieve some group purpose. Here are some suggestions to get you started:

1. First you write (or phone) friends you know who are interested in psychic development and practice. You will find that you will " just happen to meet" others who have

the same interests you have. Be sure to let others know those things you are especially expert at doing. In other words, you establish a PIP pal relationship with as many people as you wish. What you are doing is developing your own network of people with whom you can work from time to time.

2. When you have a project in mind, contact other PIPs and arrange to work on the project. For example: You want to practice mental telepathy. One of your PIP pals has expressed an interest in mental telepathy. You arrange a time that is mutually agreeable and then begin experimenting. You may agree that for the next four Saturdays at 8 p.m. you both will go to your psychic workshops. From 8 until 8:20 you will transmit a picture to your PIP pal, who will remain receptive. Then from 8:20 until 8:40 your PIP pal will transmit a picture to you while you remain receptive. At 8:40 you both leave your workshop and write down what you transmitted and what you received. Then you mail the results to each other so you each can see how well you did. Over a period of time, you will see yourself improve as a sender and as a receiver.

3. A whole group might get involved to solve a major problem. Suppose you know of a child who is seriously injured and in need of help. You contact all the PIP pals you can and give them the child's name, age, sex, and name of the town where the child lives and ask them to immediately begin sending healing, love, courage, etc., to the child. In all cases where you are helping someone, all you need to know is the name, age, sex, and town in order for your mind to quickly zero in on that individual.

4. There will be some cases where you just don't know the name, age, sex, or town. That is all right; you can still zero in on the person if you give your mind all you have about the person. An example of this is: you are driving down the highway and come upon a severe accident. The

police motion you to keep moving so you cannot stop to help. You see someone being put onto a stretcher. You immediately send love, healing, and courage to all who are injured in that accident. Your mind will be able to do that.

5. Through your PIP pals you can learn more, contribute more, and have more enjoyment than if you did not have the PIP pals. So use this opportunity. The power of collective minds is awesome.

From this point on I am going to discuss some things that you can do individually, starting immediately. Let it be understood that many of these things can also be done in concert with PIP pals.

Psychic Development Notebook
Whether you are working alone or with your own network of PIP pals, you will want to be sure to maintain complete documentation for all your work. This documentation will be valuable in helping you discover those areas of psychic work that are best suited for you and those areas that just are not for you. It also gives you concrete feedback concerning the results of your efforts. Don't just trust everything to memory—WRITE IT DOWN. Appendix B gives more complete details and suggestions concerning a recommended psychic development notebook.

Moving Cars
Have you ever been driving on the Interstate highway system and become annoyed because someone driving slowly in the fast lane was holding you up? Well, I have, and here is how I handled it. This is one you can start using right away.

Several years ago my wife and I had the need to drive to a city over a hundred miles from our home once every week. The highway was always crowded, making it a long, tedious drive. Then one day I said to my wife, "Hon, today you drive and I will move all the cars out of the way." Predictably, she thought I had a couple screws loose. "You just get in the fast lane and stay there," I assured her, "and I will keep the road clear in front of you." Being a good sport, she agreed to try it.

Within seconds after she pulled onto the highway into the fast lane she rapidly approached a car. I altered my state to theta and addressed the driver something like this, "Sir, I would be very grateful if you would kindly pull into the right-hand lane and let me pass because I have urgent need to get where I am going. Thank you."

He immediately pulled into the right lane. I mentally thanked him again as we passed.

I moved one hundred percent of the vehicles out of our way that day. Once during a clear stretch of road, I dozed off only to be awakened by my wife poking me in the ribs and saying, "Wake up. There is a truck about a half mile ahead of me." My wife was having so much fun with it that she wanted to drive on the return trip.

After a few times doing this while my wife drove, I decided to drive and see if I could also move the vehicles at the same time. It worked every time.

In nearly nine months of making these weekly trips there was only one vehicle that did not immediately respond. This story is worth telling you because it illustrates an important part of psychic work.

I was driving and an eighteen-wheeler was in front of me. I mentally projected to the driver as usual, but the driver did not respond at all. I repeated my request several more times, still no response.

Just as I was wondering why, the truck had a blowout and began to swerve all over the road. Fortunately, the driver brought the truck to a safe stop on the right shoulder of the road, but not before some terrifying swerving into both lanes for a while.

If he had pulled over to allow me to pass as I had mentally requested, I would have been alongside him when he had the blowout and there is no doubt that his truck would have slammed into my car on my wife's side.

My Higher Mind had taken care of me because I did not have the awareness to take care of myself. Apparently my mental transmission had been blocked by my Higher Mind in order to protect me. Do you see now why I had you create a shield of protection in session #3?

This mental exercise of moving vehicles out of the way greatly sharpened my telepathic sending abilities. And most importantly, it taught me how to function effectively at a psychic level with my eyes open while actively doing something.

Finding A Parking Space

After my success with moving cars, I decided to reserve parking spaces for myself just to see if I could do it. I really didn't mind having to walk some distance from my car to wherever I was going, but I just wanted to see if I could do it. Typically, just before I would leave home I would alter my consciousness to theta and visualize a parking space nearest to the door of wherever I was going (supermarket, work, etc.). I would visualize the space as being empty and having a sign on it that said "Reserved For Bill Hewitt."

Guess what? It worked every time.

Then I started to get fancy. I would reserve the third space from the door. Or the fifth, or whatever. And that worked one hundred percent of the time also.

I stopped doing this after a few months simply because I wasn't that interested in saving a few steps. But it really sharpened my visualization and psychic abilities.

Try it for yourself. It is fun and excellent development practice.

Other variations on this same theme are: having all the

traffic lights be green for you; reserving your seat at a movie.

Mental Alarm Clock

Here is a practical use of your mind that is also excellent for sharpening your psychic abilities. When you go to sleep, set your mental alarm clock to awaken you at a precise time.

Here is how you do it. When you close your eyes, and before you fall asleep, go to your psychic workshop. In your workshop visualize a clock. Move the hands of the clock to the time you want to awaken; let's say 6:58. Then mentally reaffirm, "This is the exact time I want to awaken, 6:58 a.m." Then drift off to sleep.

In the morning you will awaken quite suddenly. Immediately look at the clock. It should be 6:58. If it is within one minute or less of being 6:58, consider your exercise as being accurate. Immediately close your eyes briefly and alter your consciousness and say, "Thank you. This is the accuracy and responsiveness I desire in all my psychic work." Then open your eyes and go on about whatever you have to do.

If you are more than one minute off, do not accept that as being sufficiently accurate because that is "sloppy" psychic response. Your mind is capable of accuracy, and you must insist on it. Here is what to do about it.

First, check the accuracy of your clock. I once awakened two minutes later than I should have according to the clock. I dialed the Bureau of Standards and discovered that my clock was two minutes slow. My mind had been accurate. So don't "chew out" your mind until you have checked your clock.

If your clock is accurate, then alter your consciousness and say, "I am pleased that I was awakened. However, this is not the degree of accuracy that I demand for my psychic work. I want complete accuracy from now on. When I set my mental alarm I want to awaken exactly at the time I have chosen. I will not tolerate sloppy results." Then open your eyes and go about your business.

That night, once again set your mental alarm. Keep repeating the process nightly until you are satisfied with consistent, accurate results.

Sleep Control

When you have been driving on a long trip, have you ever gotten drowsy or even dozed off briefly at the wheel?

You can use your workshop to handle this. Here is how.

When you feel yourself becoming groggy or drowsy, immediately pull onto the shoulder of the road and stop. Close your eyes and go to your workshop. In your workshop ask your advisors to watch over you and to keep you awake until you are safely at your destination. You must be specific about your destination, such as, " . . . until I am safely at my home and in bed," or " . . . until I am in my motel room." Do not say something general such as, " . . . until I reach El Paso." I will tell you why in a moment.

Then mentally give yourself a suggestion something like this: "I am now completely rested as though I have had four hours of deep, relaxing sleep. In a few moments I am going to open my eyes and be wide awake and alert. I will remain awake and alert until I reach . . . (state your specific destination)." Then exit your workshop and continue your trip.

Here is why you should not give a general destination. If you had said " . . . until I reach El Paso" your mind would allow you to go to sleep immediately when you reached the El Paso city limits. You would be driving fifty-five miles per hour (or perhaps faster) when you reached the city limits, still many miles from your intended destination. That is no time to fall asleep.

You must be specific with the directions you give your mind.

You can use this sleep control method whenever you need to remain awake and alert for a while longer. I've used it many times to stay awake while writing late into the night.

Your Warning System

Your mind has the ability to warn you of imminent danger even though you are not consciously aware that there is a danger.

All you need to do is to go to your workshop and program in the warning signal that you want your advisors to give you to warn you of imminent danger.

A friend of mine gets warned by a flashing red light in his mind. Another one becomes extremely cold. Decide how you want to be warned and then program it in using the techniques you have already learned.

I had asked my advisors to warn me in whatever way was most appropriate for the situation. It saved my life once. Here is what happened.

I was driving about forty miles per hour on a through boulevard. My right foot, as though driven by a mind of its own, quickly jerked from the accelerator and slammed down hard on the brake pedal, bringing me to a complete emergency-type stop.

At that instant, a car shot out at high speed from a blind side street, running the stop sign in the process. He crossed just inches in front of me. Had I not stopped, there is no doubt that I would have been hit and probably killed.

It took me a few moments to recover my senses and assess the situation. From where I was I could not see down the side street because of heavy foliage. So there was no way I could have seen the speeding car approach. And I knew beyond doubt that I had not braked the car. For that brief period, some force other than my own had operated my right leg.

Health Cases

There is no greater humanitarian use of your psychic ability than to help those who are ill or injured. You received training in how to do this during the 30-session program so I won't belabor the details here.

I just want to prompt you to be ever alert for opportunities to help. If someone asks your help, do not beg off. Tell them you will do your best, and then do it!

When anyone you know is seriously ill or is injured, quietly go to your workshop and help them. You need not tell them what you are doing. In fact, you often can give more benefit if you don't tell them because they will not then consciously resist your efforts.

Do the same for strangers. You read in the newspaper that someone is badly burned in an explosion. Go to your workshop and project health, healing, freedom from unnecessary pain, courage, faith, love, etc.

All this only costs you a few minutes of your time, and it can make a tremendous difference to the one you are helping.

You gain, also. First, in knowing that you acted as a loving, responsible citizen of the universe. And secondly, because every time you use your psychic abilities they become stronger and more effective.

Develop the practice of immediately sending help, if only for a second or two, to every person you become aware of who needs help. Remember my discussion about passing the scene of an accident.

Communication With People

Communicating with people is an extremely valuable

application of your psychic abilities. It is most useful when there is some sort of barrier between you and the person with whom you wish to communicate. What you do is alter your state of consciousness and then mentally talk to, and ask questions of, the person you have in mind. Since you will be communicating with that person at their subconscious level, you will receive truthful answers and will achieve remarkable results. Here are three examples of these applications. In reality, there are probably a nearly infinite number of occasions to use this ability.

1. Ask a salesman the truth about his product. On one occasion I was dealing with a car salesman to purchase a new car. I had a strong feeling he was lying to me about the actual cost of the car and about the finance charges. But every time I asked him, he gave me a line of double-talk and vague answers so I couldn't pin him down. So I altered my consciousness and asked for the truth. I immediately got an awareness of exactly what to do to trap him.

The solution was very simple. I just took a paper and wrote down exactly what he said regarding costs and monthly payments and so forth. Then at the bottom of the paper I wrote "The above statements are one hundred percent accurate and truthful and there are no additional costs or charges of any kind. The total cost of (description of car) is ($xx,xxx)."

I then handed him the paper and asked him to sign and date it.

He refused.

So I turned and walked away while he followed me, trying to double talk his way out of it.

Of course, I did not buy from him nor have I ever gone back to that dealership.

You can avoid a lot of trouble if you use your psychic ability this way.

2. Have a frank talk with someone you are having dif-

ficulty communicating with. For example: a boss who you feel has been unreasonable or unfair; a spouse, friend, or lover with whom you have had an argument; some person who is just plain "bull-headed" about some issue.

Usually these are situations where emotions get in the way of good communication.

The solution is to go to your workshop and invite the person in. Then have a long, unemotional, frank discussion about everything. Give them a no-nonsense lecture if that seems appropriate.

This will quickly bring amazing results. You will enjoy watching the changes in other people when you use these methods. Recall that you experienced just such a situation in session #19.

Another great ploy to soften someone else's wrath or anger is to mentally send, "I love you!" over and over while they are raising hell with you. You will see them grow uneasy, start to stammer, cool down, and maybe even apologize.

3. Love, or the promise of it, is what makes the world go 'round. At some time in everyone's life there has been some person you would like to get to know but have not been able to for some reason or the other. Perhaps you were too shy. Perhaps the other person always was too busy, or maybe you just didn't know how to arrange the meeting, or whatever. Well, using your psychic ability you can get to know that "special" person.

There are several ways to work it. You can bring them into your psychic workshop and talk to them. Tell them you would like to meet them. Ask them to start paying attention to you, and so forth.

Also, every time you see them, even at a distance, mentally send a message, "Hello, my name is (your name) and I really would like to get to know you. I admire you very much and think you are an exciting person." Or use whatever message you wish.

In short order, you will get to know that person. Strange things will happen to bring it about. Some would say "coincidences" will occur. But I tell you, there is no such thing as coincidence. Everything that happens is a direct result of some energy force causing it. In these examples, it is your mental thought energy that sets the process in motion and causes the "coincidence."

One caution about using your mental powers to bring a desired "love" into your life. Be sure that is what you really want because it will happen, and you are going to have to live with it. Review my comments in session #19 about what can happen.

Communication With Entities

If you have a special interest in entities (or "ghosts" as most people refer to them) you will seek out opportunities to communicate with them. This is one of my special interests, and I take every opportunity I can to visit authentic haunted houses. I've had much enjoyment and have learned a lot by communicating with entities.

Once you start to sincerely make contact, you will find that entities will start making contact with you even though you didn't solicit it. My departed brother-in-law and departed sister-in-law have visited our house off and on for years.

In addition, you can communicate with any deceased person you wish by inviting them into your psychic workshop.

In the workshop, you have a purely intellectual contact.

In haunted places, or in occasional visits to your home, you have both a physical and spiritual presence and experience. This is something exciting. Many people are not that enthusiastic about such encounters. I am. If it titillates your fancy, go for it. You were trained for this sort of psychic experience in sessions #17 and #18.

Communication With Animals

Animals only function at those states that we call altered states. They do not have a beta state of awareness. Therefore it is easy to communicate with them. You pet lovers do it all the time whether you know it or not. The really good animal trainers do their work at a psychic level. If you have a pet, alter your state and ask your pet to come to you. Watch what happens.

In Chapter 4 I described how I used my altered state to correct our dog's health problem.

Skill Improvement

At the theta level you can visualize yourself performing a skill perfectly which will then become reality in the physical world. Say your tennis game isn't what you want it to be. Visualize yourself playing a perfect game. Do this daily and watch how your game does indeed improve. Keep up the visualization, along with your continuing to play the game, until your game is where you want it to be.

This does not mean that you can visualize yourself doing something you have never done before and then instantly become an expert at it. Not at all. Visualization will make you improve a skill you already have, or it will help you learn a skill that you don't currently have. But it will not just give you the skill without any effort on your part.

Remember, desire must always be followed with constructive action in order to become reality. There are no free rides.

Out Of Body

If having out-of-body travel with conscious awareness is something that interests you then search the library or bookstore for books on the subject so you will have a greater knowledge of the subject. Ask your Masters if this is a beneficial course for you to follow. If your Masters say "Yes," then ask them to lead you to the method for making it happen. Follow whatever your Masters direct. You may get an immediate response. Or you may be led to meet some-one who can teach you, or you may be led to a book that can teach you. Be patient, have faith and don't give up.

Reading/Studying

Your psychic ability gives you a superior way to read or study and retain and understand what you have just studied. The method is quite simple.

Alter your state of consciousness (I usually go to my workshop). Then mentally say, "In a few moments I am going to open my eyes and read (name of item you are going to read). I will have superior comprehension of what I read and I will be able to recall anything I read whenever I wish in the future." Then open your eyes and read. When you are finished reading, close your eyes and say, "I have just read (name of item) and I have superior comprehension of the material and I can recall it anytime I wish." Then open your eyes and go about whatever else you want to do. You have locked in the information for future use whenever you need it.

Psychometry

Psychometry is the ability to sense information from physical objects by touching those objects. I don't know very many people personally who can do this. I have had some success with it (refer to the murder case in Chapter 4).

The only way I know to learn this skill is to just select objects and hold or touch them. Then alter your conscious-ness and try to sense information from them. Perhaps a friend will bring you an object and not tell you who owns it or where it is from. Then try your ability to sense. Unless you are one of those rare persons who already have this natural ability, it may take some persistence to develop the skill. It is a great skill to have and it is well worth the time to develop it.

Archaeological Exploration

There are thousands of archaeological treasures still undiscovered because no one knows what they are or where to look.

If this area interests you, start mentally exploring for these treasures. When you find some, go out and physically dig them up. Or, more practically, inform a professional archaeologist who is better equipped to dig them up.

My guess is that there is at least one PIP out there who will have the special ability to find archaeological treasures.

Travel to Other Planets, Other Universes, Other Levels of Consciousness

Thought is the only known energy that does not require a measurable time to travel. Thought is instantaneous. In an instant, thought can be anywhere. This means there is absolutely no restriction as to where you can travel as a thought energy. Another universe, another planet, or any level of consciousness is as close as your properly directed thought. This is an exciting and little explored use of psychic ability. Not much has been written about it. If this is your area of interest, start now to do it. Keep accurate records of your travels. Who knows? You may have enough material to compose an interesting and valuable book from which others can learn.

The psychic training given in this book has taught you all you need to know in order to make such explorations.

I have been to Atlantis as have many others.

Solving Crimes

In Chapter 5 I described my experience in a murder case. That is the only crime I have helped with simply because that was the only one I have been asked to help solve.

I have tried to solve crimes without being asked, but have not been successful. I have found that when I am asked to do something, my psychic powers seem to intensify and become keen and I am able to perform quite well. When I do not have a request, I do not always get good results. That is just me. That is not necessarily you. So you find out for yourself what you can do.

Other things in this category are finding missing persons and missing objects.

If you know what the person or object looks like you will be able to intensify your concentration by focusing on a mental image of the person or object.

You won't know if this kind of psychic endeavor is your "cup of tea" until you try it.

Solving Problems

There are many ways to solve your daily problems. Some methods will work better for you than others, so try a number of methods several times until you find what works best for you.

Method One: Visualize the situation that you do not want as it exists. Study all the detail and then mentally say, "This is not what I want!" Then immediately erase the picture completely and replace it with a picture of exactly what you do want. Study this new picture in detail and then mentally say, "This is what I want!" Then release the whole matter to your higher mind for resolution while you go on about your business doing other things.

One common problem where you might use this approach is: you and your spouse have been quarreling and it is becoming serious. You visualize the quarreling, see the unhappy faces of you and your spouse, hear the harsh words, etc. Then you say you do not want that and erase the picture. Then immediately create a picture of you and your spouse smiling, embracing, making love, talking kindly to each other, etc. Then release that picture to your higher mind by saying that this is what you do want.

The results you get will be astounding.

Method Two: Go to your psychic workshop and fix the problem. Example: you have a cut that isn't healing as fast or as well as you want. In your workshop, remove the wound completely so that only healthy skin is there. There are many variations on using your workshop for fixing anything.

I once mentally repaired my motor home under the most adverse conditions using my workshop. Here is what happened.

My wife, our youngest daughter and her dog and I were returning from a day's outing in the Rocky Mountains in our motor home. It was late in the evening and quite dark. We were twenty miles from the next town. I was driving up the side of a steep mountain road when the engine died. My efforts to restart the engine were unsuccessful. I couldn't just stay there because of the obvious hazard, and I couldn't let the motor home roll backward down the twisting mountain road in the dark; that would be suicide. The only viable solution was to repair whatever was wrong, then start the engine and drive out of there. And I didn't have the luxury of much time to do it in. To make matters worse, I know next to nothing about vehicles other than how to drive them. My wife was becoming extremely upset. So was the dog. I had to do something.

I asked my wife and daughter to be quiet for just a few minutes. I closed my eyes and went to my psychic workshop. I brought my motor home in there along with a host of expert mechanics who I told to fix it well enough to run until I reached the next town safely. I gave them two minutes.

Then I opened my eyes and turned the key in the ignition. The engine started immediately, and I drove to the next town where the engine promptly died just as I pulled into a service station.

The service station was just closing. When I explained my problem the mechanic took a brief look at the motor home. He couldn't start it. He gave me permission to camp overnight right there in front of his gas station until the next day when the problem could be investigated more thoroughly.

The next day the mechanic found the problem. The starter motor was completely shot. Whatever was inside the starter motor was ground to bits. The mechanic poured ground metal from it. He showed me what was left of the starter. "This kind of damage couldn't occur in just a short time," he said. "There is no way you could possibly have started your engine with this starter motor." I told him about how I started it and where I had driven from the night before.

"That just is not possible," he said.

There will be times in your life when you will need to do the "impossible" just as I did that dark night on the side of the mountain. Use your psychic workshop to do it.

Method Three: Ask your Masters. I probably use this method more often than all other methods combined. Sometimes my Masters solve the problem for me. Other times they give me directions on how to solve the problem for myself. This may well be the most powerful and valuable tool you have been given in this 30-session training program . . . YOUR MASTERS.

Method Four: Dreams. You can solve your problems using your nightly dreams. When you retire for the night, alter your state of consciousness and say, "Tonight I want to have a dream that will give me information which will help me solve my problem." Mentally state your problem. Next mentally add, "I want to remember my dream when I awaken and I want to understand the meaning of the dream." Then just drift off to sleep. You will awaken either during the night or in the morning with a recollection of the dream and what it means in relation to your problem. Using dreams sometimes takes some practice. It comes fairly easily for some and is more difficult for others, so don't give up if you don't have a smashing success the first couple times you try. Persistence will pay off.

These four methods I've just described for solving problems are not the only ones, but they will do nicely. You may develop your own methods as you progress.

A Way Of Life

I could probably write another entire book about different specific ways to use your psychic abilities every day for fun, for help, for learning, for experiencing, for communicating, for discovering, for changing, for coping, and on and on. But I don't think that is necessary. I think by now I have made my point. Using your psychic abilities is a way of life. No longer are you bound by the traditional ways that you used to live by. Now you have an instantly available ability to live your life in the fullest and most exciting way possible. There is virtually nothing that you cannot handle easily, smoothly and satisfactorily. It works!

Sensitize yourself to be constantly alert for opportunities to use every psychic trick you have up your sleeve. It doesn't necessarily have to be some gigantic project (although it certainly can be) that you direct your energies toward.

You hear on the radio that a gunman is holed up in your city and he has hostages. Use your ability to project to that gunman and talk to him sensibly at the psychic level so he will not harm anyone. Project courage and protection to the hostages.

Your boss asks you to perform some demanding tasks that you aren't certain how to do. Use your psychic abilities to find out how. Solve the problem in your mind, and then do the work as your mind directs you to do. Problem solved!

You see a child crying on the street. If you are not able to stop and physically help the child, then send help and comfort at a psychic level.

I am not advocating using psychic help as a cop-out so you don't have to render physical help. Never. You should always render physical help when possible. There are thousands of times, however, when you just are not able to help physically. Then use your psychic help.

Now that you have committed yourself to a new way of life . . . the life of a daily PIP . . . there is one final piece of advice I want to impress on you.

That advice is simply this: do not become impressed with yourself. Do not go around announcing to the world or to whoever will listen, "I am a psychic. Let me butt into your business." I give this advice because I personally know psychics who have become quite egotistical and self-centered. I have seen psychics lose their abilities because they began to think that they were the source of power.

Hear this and hear it well: there is only one source of power and that is the Supreme Source that created everything. You have the privilege of being a channel for the expression of that power.

As for the cry, "I am a psychic!" So what? So is everyone, potentially. Big deal. You have merely learned how to use some of the abilities that your Creator gave you as a birthright, so don't go getting bigheaded about it.

Live your life in quiet happiness, using your power to create a better world for yourself and for all. That is what

this book and this training program are all about.
Now go forth from this moment in love and peace.

CHAPTER 7

THE ULTIMATE

Once you have completed the 30-session program exactly as described, your life will have been changed irrevocably for the better in some measure.

If you continue to practice your psychic ability every day, even if only for brief moments, the changes will continue to occur and become more profound. You are the entire play . . . the script writer . . . the actor . . . the stage manager . . . the director. You make happen those things you want to have happen. Your success rate is directly proportional to your efforts, persistence, perseverance, belief, expectancy, intensity, and openness to experience and learning.

There are a number of things you will notice happening as you become more and more in tune with your higher mind. You will have experiences that come in a flash of total awareness that nearly defies adequate description. This is because our vocabulary is designed for the physical world we are temporarily residing in, and the experiences are nonphysical. Hence, at best our physical-world words only partially embrace the needs of describing a nonphysical world. If you experience music in the psychic realm, it will be so extraordinarily profound and beautiful that you will be unable to adequately express it in words. You will see things in mental images. You will hear things in nonverbal sounds. You will gain a total awareness of something in a split second; it then may take several hours to verbally explain the information you received in that flash. And even then, you will find your explanation falling short of what you know in your mind.

Some years ago, while in meditation, I was given total awareness of reincarnation. Up until that moment, I had not read anything about reincarnation. I had not given the subject any thought. It was something I just was not interested in. In fact, I was prone to believe that there was no such thing. In this particular meditation session, I was not seeking any information about reincarnation, but I was given the information in an instant. I can now talk on the subject for some length and still not adequately explain the inner understanding and knowledge I have of the subject. The information came as a total awareness; that is the best description I am able to give. When you have your own experiences, you will understand what I am trying to say.

Another thing you will notice is that you are subtly directed into a different circle of acquaintances and relationships. Those whom you can help will be drawn to you, or you to them. Those who can help you are drawn to you, or you to them. You will be quickly weaned from those who are potentially detrimental to you. After some period of time, you will look back and find that those who were so important in your life at one time no longer are. Your life will have taken on a dimension that you could not have predicted.

Your entire value system will change. Things that used to get you uptight now will not even cause you to pause. Alcohol will not be important to you, if it ever was. You may have an occasional drink, but if you never had one you couldn't care less.

You quite likely will find cigarettes and smoke repulsive. This is due, in part at least, to the fact that you will be operating more and more in an altered state of mind both deliberately and spontaneously. In an altered state, you become extremely sensitive. Thus, smoke and cigarettes become a great irritant, and can cause physical discomfort. In my case, when in an altered state (which is most of the time for me), cigarettes or smoke anywhere near me often cause me to experience throat congestion, swelling inside my nose that blocks my breathing, and severe coughing.

Quite likely, you will become a loner in the sense that you are independent and free. You will not feel bonded to groups or rules. No one will make your decisions for you. Yet at the same time you will feel a very real spiritual bond with everyone and everything. You will see your responsibilities clearly, and you will see the responsibilities of others clearly. This is a very difficult concept to explain; you really must experience it to understand it.

It is as though you see all people as individual universes. Each is a tiny globe bubble floating through space under its own power and direction. Every so often two of these globes come together, and like bubbles, they blend and overlap. They may blend for a very short period or for a long period. While blended, these bubbles share certain portions of themselves while still maintaining their own identity and autonomy. At some point, the bubbles separate and float on to experience other bubbles. The same bubbles may come together for a while, then float apart for a while, then rejoin again, etc.

So it is with you and your interaction with others. You give experience to and gain experience from others. But you (and they) still remain the master of your own universe, and set the course for your own learning and spiritual growth. It is impossible to give without also receiving, and vice versa. A personal example may help to put some of this into perspective. Some years ago, I helped a woman (through hypnosis) to get rid of her smoking habit. She had limited funds, so I did it for just 15 percent of my usual fee. Then she went on her way out of my life.

About five years passed when I got a phone call from the woman. She was terminally ill and in the final months of her life. She was also financially destitute, but she needed help. I gave much time freely over her final months to do what I could to ease her pain, help her understand the nature of death and overcome her fears, etc. She died. I felt that my efforts had been inadequate, but didn't know what more I could have done. In the process, however, I had profound revelations of understanding and knowledge. But another payoff was yet to come.

Even though I felt I had not done much to help her, she must have felt otherwise. A few months after her death I got a phone call from a local cable television program producer who is also a significant power in certain local organizations. It seems the TV producer was a longtime friend of the lady who had died. On her deathbed, she had talked to her producer friend almost exclusively about me and the great help I had been. The TV producer was quite moved by the experience and got in touch with me. The result: I got a paid speaking engagement and commitments for several appearances on a television talk show. The kicker is that my first book was forthcoming, and this gave me the opportunity to plug it.

I could fill an entire book with just such personal experiences, but that isn't necessary to make the point: *what goes around, comes around.* You generate positive energy, and positive energy comes back to you in some way at some time. Conversely, if you generate negative energy, that too will return to you . . . count on it! There is no such thing as coincidence. Coincidence does not exist. Coincidence is one example of a physical-world word used to describe a nonphysical world experience—a woefully inadequate and inappropriate word, is it not?

Understand one thing clearly right now. Do not use your psychic abilities to help someone with the intent of receiving an ultimate reward. Such an intent is the wrong reason, and it generates negative energy which will be counterproductive to the results you expect.

Use your power to help simply because you can do it and there is a need. Just the knowledge that you did what you could is reward enough. Period. Then forget the matter and go on to other things. This will become an automatic response for you as you become more and more ingrained in the non-physical world of YOU. As a beginner, there is frequently a temptation to become greedy or selfish; resist the temptation and it will quickly pass, and your psychic development will proceed nicely.

You will not always be aware of the chain of actions that lead to an experience. Don't concern yourself about it. If you need to know, you will. In the example I just gave about the lady I helped, that chain of actions was quite evident. Most experiences are not that clearly delineated to your conscious awareness. That is why it is important to program your goals for end results and not for the specific interim steps you *think* are necessary to achieve the goals.

Years ago I programmed myself to become a successful writer. I reinforced that goal daily. I made it, but the winding, twisty, unpredictable path I was led on to get there was incredible. At any given time, it seemed highly unlikely that I was on the right path at all. Then suddenly the cloud lifted and everything fell into perspective. The unlikely path I had followed was exactly the right one, and brought rewards and experiences far beyond anything I had originally dreamed. If I had tried to program the exact path to follow, I wouldn't have had the insight to choose the one I did follow, and consequently would not have realized my goal and all the enrichment along the way. Fortunately, I had merely programmed myself for the goal, and thus gained a life experience that I would not trade with anyone for for any amount of wealth.

Each of us is an immense energy source in an infinite ocean of immense energy. This is all intelligent energy. Our awareness embraces many levels. All the knowledge, intelligence, and energy is available to us. Energy in and of itself is neither good nor bad; it just is. How we use it can be good or detrimental . . . that is our choice. Once we execute a choice, it is irrevocable, and we must deal with the results either now, in this life, or later, in another living experience. That is the Law. The Law of Being states: "Whatever comes to you, whatever happens to you, whatever surrounds you will be in accordance with your consciousness, and nothing else; that whatever is in your consciousness must happen, no matter who tries to stop it; and whatever is not in your consciousness cannot happen."

It behooves us then to make positive, beneficial, constructive choices, does it not? Use your psychic ability to go within and consult with your higher self in order to determine the best choices for you to make. You will get the guidance you need. Just be sure you lsiten and follow that small, still voice within rather than rationalize another course of action.

All of these things I tell you in this chapter will become crystal clear to you via your own inner awareness as you become more and more in tune with self at all levels of self . . . hence, oneness. Ah Ha! Oneness! Is that what this is all about, Oneness? No, not *all* about . . . rather this is the beginning of what Oneness is about. The rest you must find out and experience for yourself in your own way, at your own pace, in your own time. But the important thing is that your journey has begun, and it is an exciting one.

I tell you these things to serve as signposts along your

journey so that you may be better equipped to make wise choices. There will be times when it seems you are not progressing or are even slipping backwards. This is temporary and is necessary although you may not see why at the time. Just stick to your beliefs and goals. The Sun always rises and always prevails over the clouds, which are temporary.

We are here on Earth as part of our spiritual growth to experience ... to learn ... to contribute ... to be happy ... to achieve. We are in school, so to speak, so attend your classes, pay attention, do your homework, and look forward to passing into the next grade, and the next, and so on until you graduate.

I detect a growing awareness. You are getting a gleam in your eyes. You have the birth of an understanding. Your understanding is still an infant, but it is there and growing. You are beginning to have some insight into who you really are ... who we all are ... what life is all about ... where you are going in this Earthly existence ... where you are going ultimately.

I am not going to spell it out for you any more specifically than I have. To do so would take the edge off your own experience, and I don't want to do that.

This book provides you with a tool for greater self-realization and actualization now and always. It is within your power to enrich not only yourself, but the entire world in some measure.

Something For Everyone

The development and use of psychic ability holds something for everyone. The only limits are those which you place on yourself by not exercising your imagination or not spending some time to use your ability.

Medical professionals can use their psychic ability to aid in the diagnosis of illness. Use it to project health, healing and encouragement to patients. Use it to handle one's own stress. I know one dentist who uses his psychic ability to locate root canals with unerring accuracy; other dentists in his medical building come to him when they have difficulty locating a root canal.

Are you a shut-in? What a marvelous opportunity to project for world peace, an end to world hunger, reduction in crime, and on and on. Of course, project for your own personal goals also.

Teachers can use it to better understand students, to project knowledge mentally into fertile minds, and to better prepare themselves for class.

Writers can use their psychic ability to create better material (I conceive and write all my material in an altered state) . . . parents, to better rear their children . . . children, to better develop into responsible adults . . . athletes, to hone their skills to perfection . . . everyone to communicate with nonphysical entities . . . and so on.

If you do not know what you can best do, go to your psychic workshop and ask. You will be given direction. A number of years ago I went into my psychic workshop and asked that very question because I did not see that I was capable of anything special. Here is the answer I got: "You have the ability and responsibility to influence others. Use it wisely, and you will be guided in all you need for success." This book is one part of the charter I was given that day.

There really is no viable excuse for not using the psychic ability you were given when you were created to the fullest extent of your awareness. You know now that you have some measure of ability. You also know now how to develop it and use it. All that remains is to do it.

One Final Thought

There are several excellent ways to achieve failure, but not taking a chance is the most successful. Make your choice for success by taking a chance on doing the restructuring of your life as suggested in this book. If you do, then (to paraphrase Shakespeare):

> It must follow as the night, the day
> Thou will find success on the way.

APPENDIX A

RECOMMENDED READING

These are a few of my favorites that I recommend for your consideration. I've included a few comments about each book. There are hundreds of excellent books on the market, and new ones are coming out all the time. I do not intend this list to preclude your consideration of other fine books. *The Llewellyn New Times* also carries listings of fine books to consider.

Hypnosis by William W. Hewitt. Published by Llewellyn Publications. This is perhaps the most comprehensive book written about the use of hypnosis and self-hypnosis. It is a self-help how-to book and deals extensively with the use of the alpha state to achieve a nearly infinite number of goals. This book is the forerunner of and is closely related to *Beyond Hypnosis.*

As a Man Thinketh by James Allen. Published by DeVorss & Company. A powerful 68-page booklet that will fit into your purse or shirt pocket. It deals with how your thoughts determine your destiny.

Wisdom of The Mystic Masters by Joseph J. Weed. Published by Parker Publishing Company. Covers some of the same subjects that are covered in *Hypnosis* and *Beyond Hypnosis* plus a few other related subjects but from a different perspective.

Psycho-Cybernetics by Maxwell Maltz. Published by Wilshire Book Company. Another perspective on the whole subject of life and how to get the most out of it.

Jonathan Livingston Seagull by Richard Bach. Published by Avon. A beautiful story about the eternalness of life and the importance of living it your way and learning your lessons so you can advance spiritually.

Illusions by Richard Bach. Published by Delacorte Press. A powerful story about who you really are and your relationship to your Creator.

There's No Such Place As Far Away by Richard Bach. Published by Delacorte Press. A very short book about love, life, and time told in a sort of fairy-tale way.

A Warm Fuzzy Tale by Claude Steiner. Published by Jalmar Press. A fairy tale about the positive and negative influences in life. A powerful story, beautifully told. For all ages. I love it.

The Little Prince by Antoine De Saint-Exupery. Published by Harcourt, Brace & World, Inc. A beautiful fairy tale for all ages that will give you a perspective of life that you had never before considered. I love this one, too.

Any of the books by Emmet Fox. Here are six, published by Harper & Row, that I especially recommend:

Make Your Life Worthwhile
The Ten Commandments
The Sermon On The Mount
Power Through Constructive Thinking
Find and Use Your Inner Power
Around the Year With Emmet Fox

Emmet Fox is my very favorite of all metaphysical writers. He has an easy-to-read style, and he covers very deep, profound subjects in a way that is easy to understand. For those of you who want to expand your consciousness to embrace ALL, Emmet Fox is a "must" on your reading list. Fox's books will probably have more significance for you if you wait until you have developed your own psychic abilities for a year or so.

The preceding list has something for everyone in helping you develop, expand, understand, and use your consciousness.

Following are two very good books for those of you with special interests. Neither of these books relates to your development. They serve only to provide more knowledge in certain areas if you are interested in those areas.

The Airmen Who Would Not Die by John G. Fuller. Published by G.P. Putnam's Sons. This is an exciting and well-documented factual account of life after death. It is taken from various British "official" records that are beyond dispute.

Psychic Discoveries Behind The Iron Curtain by Sheila Ostrander and Lynn Schroeder. Published by Bantam Books. The title tells what it is all about. Interesting and informative.

APPENDIX B

PSYCHIC DEVELOPMENT NOTEBOOK

Your psychic development and experience are ongoing processes for life. It helps a great deal, especially in the early development stages, to maintain a psychic notebook. Record in your notebook all of your psychic experiences and experiments.

With a notebook you can quickly ascertain what you can do best, where your natural talents lie, what interests you most, and least, which methods work best for you, etc. Armed with the resultant information, you can then zero in on exactly which psychic paths are best for you to pursue.

This appendix suggests some of the content ideas for such a notebook. Exactly how you format and organize the notebook is your choice.

DREAMS: In this notebook section write down all of the details you can recall from all of your dreams. Also write down what your interpretation of each dream is. Be sure to write the date of the dreams. If there were several dreams in one night, make note of the sequence.

Was the dream spontaneous or was it one you deliberately programmed yourself for? If programmed, write down the programming method you used—put in complete detail.

Record your dreams as soon as possible—hopefully immediately—after you recall them. Dream detail quickly fades, so don't put it off "until later in the day."

TELEPATHY: Record all of your telepathic experiences, including the dates and time of day.

Was it spontaneous, such as knowing who was phoning you before you picked up the phone?

Was it an experiment, such as trying to read someone else's thoughts, read a deck of cards, etc.?

Did you do the experiment alone or with someone else? If with someone else, record their name and physical location at the time.

When working with someone else, record those times when you were a sender and a receiver. Give complete detail. This will help you determine if you are better at receiving or sending.

Make detailed notes of the procedures you use and those of others working with you. Always describe the results so you can learn and improve.

HEALING: Record names, dates, time of day, type of illness or problem.

Was the healing in person? Laying on of hands? Using crystals? At a distance using mental projection? Was the person being healed aware at the time?

Describe exactly what you did. What were the results? Did one-time healing get the job done or were several times needed over some period of time?

CHANNELING: Date and time of day. Physical location. Names of all persons present. Names of all entities contacted. Complete detail of all messages channeled and of all questions asked. Exactly what did you do to prepare yourself for the channeling?

Were you consciously aware of what was happening at

the time? Did you remember afterwards?

Were you in a trance state with no personal awareness of what transpired? How were all events recorded? Maintain accuracy and completeness.

PROPHESY: Record all your prophesies, giving all times, dates, names, details, etc. Record when the prophesy you made was well and what the prophesy was. Put names of witnesses, if any.

Was it spontaneous—did it just come to you? Did you use a specific programming procedure to enable you to make prophesies? What were the procedures?

Keep track of the accuracy of your predictions.

TELEKINESIS: What procedure did you use to move, or attempt to move, an object? What object? When? Under what circumstances? Any witnesses? Who? Results? Put it all down in your notebook.

GHOSTS: Record all of the what, why, when, how, where, and who of this exciting psychic experience. Where you can verify information, do so and record it.

PAST LIFE REGRESSION: This section might well be in its own notebook because of the large volume of information you might collect. As with all psychic work, record every last bit of detail and always record dates, time of day, names, places, etc. Verify as much information as you can from regression experiences. If regression is your specialty, it will give hours of pleasure and information. Be sure to specify what regression techniques you use.

MEDITATION: There will be times when you do not have any specific things you wish to do. You just want to relax, unwind, tune in to higher intelligence and listen. This is meditation, and it may be the best psychic practice of all because it enables you to gain great knowledge and insight, to maintain perspective and balance, and to take counsel with cosmic intelligence.

I strongly recommend you meditate at least once a day

even if only for a few minutes. Profound things can sometimes happen during meditation.

Record in your notebook the details of the various meditation techniques you may use. Write down afterwards what happened during meditation. As always, include date and time of meditation. Much of the time you will simply record that you just felt relaxed, peaceful, and good—there won't be anything else to report. But every once in a while—ZAP! A profound experience is given to you.

One day I was meditating just to relax—it had been an especially hectic day. Suddenly I was given complete knowledge of reincarnation in a brilliant flash of awareness. Ultimately, this knowledge led to my creation of a new past-life regression technique that I now have published on two cassette tapes.

So document all of your meditation experiences—they are valuable.

SUMMARY: The nine psychic avenues I've just talked about are by no means all there is. This is just to give you an idea.

You may want to move cars on the freeway or save parking spaces such as I've described elsewhere in this book. Of course record time, date, place and results.

And there are: tarot cards, tea leaf reading, I Ching, ouija board, clairvoyance, clairaudience, psychometry and on and on.

Whatever you choose to try, make complete records. Eventually you will become aware of what you are best at or what interests you most.

Expect to get no results from some things—perhaps telepathy doesn't work for you but tea leaf reading does. And so forth.

Eventually you will make your own decision on the two or three things you prefer to pursue and will stop spending time on the other things.

Be happy for those things you can do. Do not fret over those things you seem unable to do. Some things you can do better than others. That is just the way it is. Accept it. You are who you are.

You are unique. Capitalize on your uniqueness and create a better life for yourself and others.

Good luck!

STAY IN TOUCH

On the following pages you will find listed, with their current prices, some of the books now available on related subjects. Your book dealer stocks most of these, and will stock new titles in the Llewellyn series as they become available. We urge your patronage.

However, to obtain our full catalog, to keep informed of new titles as they are released and to benefit from informative articles and helpful news, you are invited to write for our bi-monthly news magazine/catalog. A sample copy is free, and it will continue coming to you at no cost as long as you are an active mail customer. Or you may keep it coming for a full year with a donation of just $5.00 in U.S.A. & Canada ($20.00 overseas, first class mail). Many bookstores also have *The Llewellyn New Times* available to their customers. Ask for it.

Stay in touch! In *The Llewellyn New Times'* pages you will find news and reviews of new books, tapes and services, announcements of meetings and seminars, articles helpful to our readers, news of authors, advertising of products and services, special money-making opportunities, and much more.

The Llewellyn New Times
P.O. Box 64383-Dept. 305, St. Paul, MN 55164-0383, U.S.A.
• • •
TO ORDER BOOKS AND TAPES

If your book dealer does not have the books described on the following pages readily available, you may order them direct from the publisher by sending full price in U.S. funds, plus $1.50 for postage and handling for orders *under* $10.00; $3.00 for orders *over* $10.00. There are no postage and handling charges for orders over $50. UPS Delivery: We ship UPS whenever possible. Delivery guaranteed. Provide your street address as UPS does not deliver to P.O. Boxes. UPS to Canada requires a $50 minimum order. Allow 4–6 weeks for delivery. Orders outside the U.S.A. and Canada: Airmail—add retail price of book; add $5 for each non-book item (tapes, etc.); add $1 per item for surface mail.

FOR GROUP STUDY AND PURCHASE

Because there is a great deal of interest in group discussion and study of the subject matter of this book, we feel that we should encourage the adoption and use of this particular book by such groups by offering a special "quantity" price to group leaders or "agents."

Our Special Quantity Price for a minimum order of five copies of *Beyond Hypnosis* is $23.85 cash-with-order. This price includes postage and handling within the United States. Minnesota residents must add 6.5% sales tax. For additional quantities, please order in multiples of five. For Canadian and foreign orders, add postage and handling charges as above. Credit card (VISA, Master Card, American Express) orders are accepted. Charge card orders only may be phoned free ($15.00 minimum order) within the U.S.A. or Canada by dialing 1-800-THE-MOON. Customer service calls dial 1-612-291-1970. Mail Orders to:

LLEWELLYN PUBLICATIONS
P.O. Box 64383-Dept. 305, St. Paul, MN 55164-0383, U.S.A.

Prices subject to change without notice.

TEA LEAF READING
by William W. Hewitt
There may be more powerful methods of divination than tea leaf reading, but they also require heavy-duty commitment and disciplined training. Fun, lighthearted, and requiring very little discipline, tea leaf reading asks only of its practitioners an open mind and a spirit of adventure.

Just one cup of tea can give you a 12-month prophecy, or an answer to a specific question. It can also be used to examine the past. There is no regimen needed, no complicated rules to memorize. Simply read the instructions and look up the meanings of the symbols!

Tea Leaf Reading explains the hows: how it works; how to prepare the cup for reading; how to analyze and read tea leaf symbols; how to interpret the symbols you see. It provides an extensive glossary of symbols with their meanings so you can begin interpretations immediately; it provides an index, with cross-references for quick location of the symbols in the glossary; and it has an appendix of crystals and metals that can aid you in reading tea leaves and in other pursuits.

Tea Leaf Reading is the trailblazer on the subject—there are no other books like it!

0-87542-308-6, 240 pgs., mass market $3.95

HYPNOSIS: A Power Program for Self-Improvement
by William Hewitt
There is no other hypnosis book on the market that has the depth, scope, and explicit detail as does this book. The exact and complete wording of dozens of hypnosis routines is given. Real case histories and examples are included for a broad spectrum of situations. Precise instructions for achieving self-hypnosis, the alpha state, and theta state are given. There are dozens of hypnotic suggestions given covering virtually any type of situation one might encounter. The book tells how to become a professional hypnotist. It tells how to become expert at self-hypnosis all by yourself without external help. And it even contains a short dissertation going "beyond hypnosis" into the realm of psychic phenomena. There is something of value here for nearly everyone.

This book details exactly how to gain all you want—to enrich your life at every level. No matter how simple or how profound your goals, this book teaches you how to realize them. The book is not magic; it is a powerful key to unlock the magic within each of us.

0-87542-300-0, 192 pgs., 5¼ x 8, softcover $6.95

THE LLEWELLYN PRACTICAL GUIDE
TO CREATIVE VISUALIZATION
by Denning & Phillips

All things you will ever want must have their start in your mind. The average person uses very little of the full creative power that is his, potentially. It's like the power locked in the atom—it's all there, but you have to learn to release it and apply it constructively.

IF YOU CAN SEE IT... in your Mind's Eye ... you will have it! It's true: you can have whatever you want—but there are "laws" to mental creation that must be followed. The power of the mind is not limited to, nor limited by, the material world—Creative Visualization enables Man to reach beyond, into the invisible world of Astral and Spiritual Forces.

Some people apply this innate power without actually knowing what they are doing, and achieve great success and happiness; most people, however, use this same power, again unknowingly, incorrectly, and experience bad luck, failure, or at best an unfulfilled life.
This book changes that. Through an easy series of step-by-step, progressive exercises, your mind is applied to bring desire into realization! Wealth, power, success, happiness even psychic powers ... even what we call magickal power and spiritual attainment ... all can be yours. You can easily develop this completely natural power, and correctly apply it, for your immediate and practical benefit. Illustrated with unique,"puts-you-into-the-picture" visualization aids.

0-87542-183-0, 294 pgs., 5-1/4 x 8, illus., softcover $8.95

THE LLEWELLYN PRACTICAL GUIDE TO
THE DEVELOPMENT OF PSYCHIC POWERS
by Denning & Phillips

You may not realize it, but you already have the ability to use ESP, Astral Vision and Clairvoyance, Divination, Dowsing, Prophecy, Communication with Spirits, to exercise (as with any talent) and develop them.

Written by two of the most knowledgeable experts in the world of Magick today, this book is a complete course—teaching you, step-by-step, how to develop these powers that actually have been yours since birth. Using the techniques they teach, you will soon be able to move objects at a distance, see into the future, know the thoughts and feelings of another person, find lost objects, locate water and even people using your own no-longer latent talents.

Psychic powers are as much a natural ability as any other talent. You'll learn to play with these new skills, work with groups of friends to accomplish things you never would have believed possible before reading this book. The text shows you how to make the equipment you can use, the exercises you can do—many of them at any time, anywhere—and how to use your abilities to change your life and the lives of those close to you. Many of the exercises are presented in forms that can be adapted as games for pleasure and fun, as well as development.
0-87542-191-1, 256 pgs., 5-1/4 x 8, illus., softcover $8.95

Prices subject to change without notice.